Encounters with Jesus in John's Gospel

A Workbook

by
James J. Stewart

Illustrated by Jenn Kokal

© 2021 James J. Stewart
ISBN: 978-1-7362724-4-2

All Biblical quotations are from:
The World English Bible [WEB]
Derived from the *American Standard Version* ©1901
Published by Rainbow Missions, Public Domain (Copyright waived)

Holiness, like prayer (which is indeed part of it), is something that, though Christians have an instinct for it through their new birth, as we shall see, they have to learn in and through experience.

Packer, J. I., *Rediscovering Holiness* (p. 14). Baker Publishing Group. Kindle Edition.

Table of Contents

Introduction 6
Chapter One 9
Chapter Two 13
Chapter Three 16
Chapter Four 19
Chapter Five 23
Chapter Six 28
Chapter Seven 34
Chapter Eight 41
Chapter Nine 47
Chapter Ten 50
Chapter Eleven 54
Chapter Twelve 59
Chapter Thirteen 65
Chapter Fourteen 71
Chapter Fifteen 78
Chapter Sixteen 82
Chapter Seventeen 86
Chapter Eighteen 89
Chapter Nineteen 94
Chapter Twenty 101
Chapter Twenty-one 105
Other Books by the Author 111

Introduction

As a spiritual and theological way of seeing Jesus, we can think of our Savior as being the human window through whom we see God. The closer we get to a window, the more we see what's beyond the window. Jesus said, "… He who has seen me has seen the Father…." (John 14:9b (WEB]) This statement gives us a glimpse of Jesus' holiness and character.

1 Peter 1:15 [WEB] says, "… but just as he who called you is holy, you yourselves also be holy in all of your behavior…." John's Gospel gives us many examples of Jesus' character and holiness. When we look at these encounters carefully, there is much we can learn. In most instances today, we like our holiness at a distance. Just as surely as we believe in government cutbacks, except in our backyard, we believe in discipline and rigid standards for the other guy, and we believe in mercy for ourselves. Some non-Christians don't want a preacher living next door. When we faithfully follow Jesus and try to be like Him, we should have a good attitude toward holiness. In the original languages of the Bible, holiness refers to being set apart for God, consecrated and surrendered to Him. In a very practical way, to grow towards our savior's holiness means to be a spiritually faithful reflection of Jesus. Encounters with Jesus in John's gospel lead to growth in holiness. We can see it in the apostles, and we can gain it in ourselves.

In the New Testament, there are traditionally four books about the life, death and resurrection of Jesus, our Savior. These four books are located at the start of the New Testament and are known as the Gospels. The word gospel means good news. The New Testament starts with the Gospel of Matthew, followed by that of Mark, Luke, and John. While the Gospels of Matthew, Mark and Luke have numerous parallel passages, the Gospel of John is different. John the Apostle was the youngest of the twelve who were close to Jesus. John's gospel includes fewer accounts of Jesus' public teachings than the gospels of Matthew, Mark, and Luke, but John includes more of what Jesus said in conversations with individuals and small groups. So, there are relatively few direct parallels with the Gospel of John in the other three Gospels. In John, we can observe those closest to Jesus growing towards Jesus' holiness.

John's gospel was written late in the first century after the other gospels were already in circulation. John had no need to reproduce this material, and he chose to write from a more personal point of view. The evidence in the four Gospels indicates that John was remarkably close to Jesus. Maybe it was because John was the youngest and most inexperienced in life, so that Jesus could be especially attentive to always include him in all that happened.

This book sets up encounters with Jesus with a simple approach.

1. Read a few verses of the World English Bible that are provided. (You can also use the version or translation you like best.) Notes are provided in this workbook to aid readers in understanding. Similar notes can be found on Annotated Bibles and Study Bibles.
2. These are followed by questions for reflection, prayer, and discussion. There are not necessarily 'good' or 'bad' answers to these questions. The questions help the reader ponder the character and holiness of Jesus. Some of the questions inspire the faithful disciples of Jesus to think of holiness and to grow towards holiness seen in Jesus.

You do not need to have an extensive knowledge of the Bible or of Jesus to have encounters with Jesus through this book. Small groups can schedule times for discussion by the whole group. As we read the Bible all the time, there is often a way for it to change us. It is because faithfully following Jesus and attempting to be like Him means growing and changing spiritually. While it does not mean achieving Jesus' holiness, it does mean growing towards His holiness and reflecting it as best we can as we faithfully follow Him and try to be like Him. Be sure you use a translation and not a paraphrase, as a modern paraphrase of the Bible is usually not useful for serious study or for spiritual growth.

Chapter One
God's Holiness Descends to Earth in Jesus

 **A Cosmic Vision**

John 1:1-18 [WEB]

1. In the beginning was the Word, and the Word was with God, and the Word was God. 2 The same was in the beginning with God. 3 All things were made through him. Without him, nothing was made that has been made. 4 In him was life, and the life was the light of men. 5 The light shines in the darkness, and the darkness hasn't overcome it. 6 There came a man sent from God, whose name was John. 7 The same came as a witness, that he might testify about the light, that all might believe through him. 8 He was not the light, but was sent that he might testify about the light. 9 The true light that enlightens everyone was coming into the world. 10 He was in the world, and the world was made through him, and the world didn't recognize him. 11 He came to his own, and those who were his own didn't receive him. 12 But as many as received him, to them he gave the right to become God's children, to those who believe in his name: 13 who were born, not of blood, nor of the will of the flesh, nor of the will of man, but of God. 14 The Word became flesh and lived among us. We saw his glory, such glory as of the only born Son of the Father, full of grace and truth. 15 John testified about him. He cried out, saying, "This was he of whom I said, 'He who comes after me has surpassed me, for he was before me.' " 16 From his fullness we all received grace upon grace. 17 For the law was given through Moses. Grace and truth were realized through Jesus Christ. 18 No one has seen God at any time. The only born Son, who is in the bosom of the Father, has declared him.

Notes

1. Instead of starting with the life of Jesus on Earth, the Gospel of John dates back to the beginning of creation, parallel to Genesis.
2. In his gospel, John gives a new meaning to the Greek word, *logos*, which is translated '**word**.' For John and his gospel, that means more than mere words. The word of God is action: to create, transmute, change, and redeem. A direct comparison may be made with the story of creation in Genesis, where, when God speaks, the result is creation itself.
3. In becoming flesh in the person of Jesus, John says that the promises of God (the word of God) are fulfilled.
4. Light was often associated with the truth and wisdom of the Biblical world.
5. With "The Word became flesh and made his dwelling among us," [14] John's original readers received a poignant picture. A literal translation of the Greek can be that He ***"pitched tent with us."***
6. God's grace is now unlimited ["grace upon grace"], as is God's fidelity [truth], and God's intimacy with us [the Father's heart].

Questions for Reflection, Prayer, and Discussion

1. Why is it important to give one's word for something?

2. Since John does not provide a birth story like Matthew and Luke, what does this scripture tell you about the origin of Jesus?

3. Since Jesus is fully God and fully human, what qualities do you expect from him that makes him holy and not just a man?

Read in your Bible: Jesus' Cousin Testifies
John 1:19-34 [WEB]

19 This is John's testimony, when the Jews sent priests and Levites from Jerusalem to ask him, "Who are you?"

20 He declared, and didn't deny, but he declared, "I am not the Christ."

21 They asked him, "What then? Are you Elijah?"

He said, "I am not."

"Are you the prophet?"

He answered, "No."

22 They said therefore to him, "Who are you? Give us an answer to take back to those who sent us. What do you say about yourself?"

23 He said, "I am the voice of one crying in the wilderness, 'Make straight the way of the Lord,' as Isaiah the prophet said."

24 The ones who had been sent were from the Pharisees. 25 They asked him, "Why then do you baptize if you are not the Christ, nor Elijah, nor the prophet?"

26 John answered them, "I baptize in water, but among you stands one whom you don't know. 27 He is the one who comes after me, who is preferred before me, whose sandal strap I'm not worthy to loosen."

28 These things were done in Bethany beyond the Jordan, where John was baptizing.

29 The next day, he saw Jesus coming to him, and said, "Behold, the Lamb of God, who takes away the sin of the world! 30 This is he of whom I said, 'After me comes a man who is preferred before me, for he was before me.' 31 I didn't know him, but for this reason I came baptizing in water, that he would be revealed to Israel." 32 John testified, saying, "I have seen the Spirit descending like a dove out of heaven, and it remained on him. 33 I didn't recognize him, but he who sent me to baptize in water said to me, 'On whomever you will see the Spirit descending and remaining on him is he who baptizes in the Holy Spirit.' 34 I have seen and have testified that this is the Son of God."

Notes
1. The expectation was that Elijah would return before the arrival of the Messiah. Jesus later attributes that to him.
2. Isaiah, by virtue of his prophecies, was also extensively associated with the coming of the Messiah.
3. Until John the baptist, baptism was associated with conversion to a new religion rather than John's appeal for repentance.

Questions for Reflection, Prayer, and Discussion
1. Between living John's way of life or Jesus' way of life, why does Jesus' way of life appear more attractive?

2. What are some of the benefits of living a life of self-imposed poverty, like John the Baptist lived?

3. When John says that Jesus baptizes with the Holy Spirit, what do you think that means?

READ: The First Followers Encounter Jesus
John 1:35-51 [WEB]

35 Again, the next day, John was standing with two of his disciples, 36 and he looked at Jesus as he walked, and said, "Behold, the Lamb of God!" 37 The two disciples heard him speak, and they followed Jesus. 38 Jesus turned and saw them following, and said to them, "What are you looking for?"

They said to him, "Rabbi" (which is to say, being interpreted, Teacher), "where are you staying?"

39 He said to them, "Come and see."

They came and saw where he was staying, and they stayed with him that day. It was about the tenth hour. 40 One of the two who heard John and followed him was Andrew, Simon Peter's brother. 41 He first found his own brother, Simon, and said to him, "We have found the Messiah!" (which is, being interpreted, Christ). 42 He brought him to Jesus. Jesus looked at him and said, "You are Simon the son of Jonah. You shall be called Cephas" (which is by interpretation, Peter). 43 On the next day, he was determined to go out into Galilee, and he found Philip. Jesus said to him, "Follow me." 44 Now Philip was from Bethsaida, the city of Andrew and Peter. 45 Philip found Nathanael, and said to him, "We have found him of whom Moses in the law and also the prophets, wrote: Jesus of Nazareth, the son of Joseph."

46 Nathanael said to him, "Can any good thing come out of Nazareth?"

Philip said to him, "Come and see."

47 Jesus saw Nathanael coming to him, and said about him, "Behold, an Israelite indeed, in whom is no deceit!"

48 Nathanael said to him, "How do you know me?"

Jesus answered him, "Before Philip called you, when you were under the fig tree, I saw you."

49 Nathanael answered him, "Rabbi, you are the Son of God! You are King of Israel!"

50 Jesus answered him, "Because I told you, 'I saw you underneath the fig tree,' do you believe? You will see greater things than these!" 51 He said to him, "Most certainly, I tell you all, hereafter you will see heaven opened, and the angels of God ascending and descending on the Son of Man."

Notes

1. Philip and Nathaniel appear to experience and respond to the holiness of Jesus.
2. It is generally assumed that Nathaniel is the same person as Bartholomew in the other three Gospels, though this is by no means certain.
3. The name, Peter, means "rock" or "rocky."

Questions for Reflection, Prayer, and Discussion

1. What qualities could Jesus have seen in Peter that caused him to rename him "Rocky?"

2. What "holy" qualities could Nathanael have seen in Jesus who made him abandon all to follow him?

Chapter Two
Christ's Holiness Blesses

ReAD in your Bible <u>A Wedding's Miracle Gift</u>
John 2:1-12 [WEB]

1 The third day, there was a wedding in Cana of Galilee. Jesus' mother was there. 2 Jesus also was invited, with his disciples, to the wedding. 3 When the wine ran out, Jesus' mother said to him, "They have no wine."

4 Jesus said to her, "Woman, what does that have to do with you and me? My hour has not yet come."

5 His mother said to the servants, "Whatever he says to you, do it."

6 Now there were six water pots of stone set there after the Jews' way of purifying, containing two or three metretes apiece. 7 Jesus said to them, "Fill the water pots with water." So they filled them up to the brim. 8 He said to them, "Now draw some out, and take it to the ruler of the feast." So they took it. 9 When the ruler of the feast tasted the water now become wine, and didn't know where it came from (but the servants who had drawn the water knew), the ruler of the feast called the bridegroom 10 and said to him, "Everyone serves the good wine first, and when the guests have drunk freely, then that which is worse. You have kept the good wine until now!" 11 This beginning of his signs Jesus did in Cana of Galilee, and revealed his glory; and his disciples believed in him.

12 After this, he went down to Capernaum, he, and his mother, his brothers, and his disciples; and they stayed there a few days.

Notes
1. Mary knows Jesus' holiness and exercises her knowledge as His mother.
2. Cana is a small village northwest of Nazareth.
3. Jesus' address of Mary translated simply as *woman* was a Greek word used with respect in that culture.
4. Jesus affirms [4] that the time for His being made known as Messiah was to be determined by God – not even by His mother's needs or desires. The celebration may go on for several days.
5. John's term, signs, denotes the events that manifest God's power present in Jesus.

Questions for Reflection, Prayer, and Discussion
1. Although Mary seems to ask her Son a little too much, why do you think Jesus answered as he did?

2. If you were present for this first of His miracles, and recognized it as a miracle, what effect could it have upon you?

3. Do you think the servants who knew the water had been turned into wine may have thought that Jesus was somehow holy?

READ in your Bible — An Encounter of Righteous Anger
John 2:13-25 [WEB]

13 The Passover of the Jews was at hand, and Jesus went up to Jerusalem. 14 He found in the temple those who sold oxen, sheep, and doves, and the changers of money sitting. 15 He made a whip of cords and drove all out of the temple, both the sheep and the oxen; and he poured out the changers' money and overthrew their tables. 16 To those who sold the doves, he said, "Take these things out of here! Don't make my Father's house a marketplace!" 17 His disciples remembered that it was written, "Zeal for your house will eat me up."

18 The Jews therefore answered him, "What sign do you show us, seeing that you do these things?"

19 Jesus answered them, "Destroy this temple, and in three days I will raise it up."

20 The Jews therefore said, "It took forty-six years to build this temple! Will you raise it up in three days?" 21 But he spoke of the temple of his body. 22 When therefore he was raised from the dead, his disciples remembered that he said this, and they believed the Scripture and the word which Jesus had said.

23 Now when he was in Jerusalem at the Passover, during the feast, many believed in his name, observing his signs which he did. 24 But Jesus didn't entrust himself to them, because he knew everyone, 25 and because he didn't need for anyone to testify concerning man; for he himself knew what was in man.

Notes
1. The temple tax was paid with Jewish money, so Roman currency had to be converted.
2. The animals were utilized for sacrifice.

Questions for Reflection, Prayer, and Discussion
1. Was it a flash of character, or did Jesus express righteousness?

2. Was Jesus out of control?

3. As John was writing his gospel as an old man, do you think he had a full understanding of who Jesus was in terms of being fully human and fully God?

Chapter Three
Holiness is Humbling

READ <u>A Clandestine Encounter by an Authority:</u>
<u>John 3:1-21 [WEB]</u>

1 Now there was a man of the Pharisees named Nicodemus, a ruler of the Jews. 2 He came to Jesus by night and said to him, "Rabbi, we know that you are a teacher come from God, for no one can do these signs that you do, unless God is with him."

3 Jesus answered him, "Most certainly I tell you, unless one is born anew, he can't see God's Kingdom."

4 Nicodemus said to him, "How can a man be born when he is old? Can he enter a second time into his mother's womb and be born?"

5 Jesus answered, "Most certainly I tell you, unless one is born of water and Spirit, he can't enter into God's Kingdom. 6 That which is born of the flesh is flesh. That which is born of the Spirit is spirit. 7 Don't marvel that I said to you, 'You must be born anew.' 8 The wind blows where it wants to, and you hear its sound, but don't know where it comes from and where it is going. So is everyone who is born of the Spirit."

9 Nicodemus answered him, "How can these things be?"

10 Jesus answered him, "Are you the teacher of Israel, and don't understand these things? 11 Most certainly I tell you, we speak that which we know and testify of that which we have seen, and you don't receive our witness. 12 If I told you earthly things and you don't believe, how will you believe if I tell you heavenly things? 13 No one has ascended into heaven but he who descended out of heaven, the Son of Man, who is in heaven. 14 As Moses lifted up the serpent in the wilderness, even so must the Son of Man be lifted up, 15 that whoever believes in him should not perish, but have eternal life. 16 For God so loved the world, that he gave his only born Son, that whoever believes in him should not perish, but have eternal life. 17 For God didn't send his Son into the world to judge the world, but that the world should be saved through him. 18 He who believes in him is not judged. He who doesn't believe has been judged already, because he has not believed in the name of the only born Son of God. 19 This is the judgment, that the light has come into the world, and men loved the darkness rather than the light, for their works were evil. 20 For everyone who does evil hates the light and doesn't come to the light, lest his works would be exposed. 21 But he who does the truth comes to the light, that his works may be revealed, that they have been done in God."

Notes

1. The Pharisees were totally devoted to The Torah [law] and to the keeping of it.
2. Rebirth by Baptism was a widely understood concept. When people baptized into Judaism, they even got a new name as a confirmation of their completely new life.
3. The reference to Moses appears in Numbers 21:9.

Questions for Reflection, Prayer, and Discussion

1. What do you say if somebody says they believe they're going to heaven because they're good?

2. When you were baptized, did you emerge from the water with the impression of being a new person?

3. If Nicodemus had at least some sense of the holiness of Jesus, why might Nicodemus think Jesus was different?

ReAD in your Bible — More Testimony from Jesus' Cousin:
John 3:22-36 [WEB]

22 After these things, Jesus came with his disciples into the land of Judea. He stayed there with them and baptized. 23 John also was baptizing in Enon near Salim, because there was much water there. They came and were baptized; 24 for John was not yet thrown into prison. 25 Therefore a dispute arose on the part of John's disciples with some Jews about purification. 26 They came to John and said to him, "Rabbi, he who was with you beyond the Jordan, to whom you have testified, behold, he baptizes, and everyone is coming to him."

27 John answered, "A man can receive nothing unless it has been given him from heaven. 28 You yourselves testify that I said, 'I am not the Christ,' but, 'I have been sent before him.' 29 He who has the bride is the bridegroom; but the friend of the bridegroom, who stands and hears him, rejoices greatly because of the bridegroom's voice. Therefore my joy is made full. 30 He must increase, but I must decrease.

31 "He who comes from above is above all. He who is from the earth belongs to the earth and speaks of the earth. He who comes from heaven is above all. 32 What he has seen and heard, of that he testifies; and no one receives his witness. 33 He who has received his witness has set his seal to this, that God is true. 34 For he whom God has sent speaks the words of God; for God gives the Spirit without measure. 35 The Father loves the Son, and has given all things into his hand. 36 One who believes in the Son has eternal life, but one who disobeys the Son won't see life, but the wrath of God remains on him."

Notes

1. Purification was a significant ceremonial element in the Jewish religion.
2. Israel is the bride, Jesus the groom, and John is the groomsman.

Questions for Reflection, Prayer, and Discussion

1. As a prophet, do you believe that John knew his cousin well and understood clearly who Jesus was?

2. Why would somebody who heard and saw Jesus return to John with questions?

Chapter Four
Holiness Is Encompassing

READ **An Encounter in Samaria**
John 4:1-42 [WEB]

1 Therefore when the Lord knew that the Pharisees had heard that Jesus was making and baptizing more disciples than John 2 (although Jesus himself didn't baptize, but his disciples), 3 he left Judea and departed into Galilee. 4 He needed to pass through Samaria. 5 So he came to a city of Samaria called Sychar, near the parcel of ground that Jacob gave to his son Joseph. 6 Jacob's well was there. Jesus therefore, being tired from his journey, sat down by the well. It was about the sixth hour. 7 A woman of Samaria came to draw water. Jesus said to her, "Give me a drink." 8 For his disciples had gone away into the city to buy food.

9 The Samaritan woman therefore said to him, "How is it that you, being a Jew, ask for a drink from me, a Samaritan woman?" (For Jews have no dealings with Samaritans.)

10 Jesus answered her, "If you knew the gift of God, and who it is who says to you, 'Give me a drink,' you would have asked him, and he would have given you living water."

11 The woman said to him, "Sir, you have nothing to draw with, and the well is deep. So where do you get that living water? 12 Are you greater than our father Jacob, who gave us the well and drank from it himself, as did his children and his livestock?"

13 Jesus answered her, "Everyone who drinks of this water will thirst again, 14 but whoever drinks of the water that I will give him will never thirst again; but the water that I will give him will become in him a well of water springing up to eternal life."

15 The woman said to him, "Sir, give me this water, so that I don't get thirsty, neither come all the way here to draw."

16 Jesus said to her, "Go, call your husband, and come here."

17 The woman answered, "I have no husband."

Jesus said to her, "You said well, 'I have no husband,' 18 for you have had five husbands; and he whom you now have is not your husband. This you have said truly."

19 The woman said to him, "Sir, I perceive that you are a prophet. 20 Our fathers worshiped in this mountain, and you Jews say that in Jerusalem is the place where people ought to worship."

21 Jesus said to her, "Woman, believe me, the hour is coming when neither in this mountain nor in Jerusalem will you worship the Father. 22 You worship that which you don't know. We worship that which we know; for salvation is from the Jews. 23 But the hour comes, and now is, when the true worshipers will worship the Father in spirit and truth, for the Father seeks such to be his worshipers. 24 God is spirit, and those who worship him must worship in spirit and truth."

25 The woman said to him, "I know that Messiah is coming, he who is called Christ. When he has come, he will declare to us all things."

26 Jesus said to her, "I am he, the one who speaks to you."

27 Just then, his disciples came. They marveled that he was speaking with a woman; yet no one said, "What are you looking for?" or, "Why do you speak with her?" 28 So the woman left her water pot, went

away into the city, and said to the people, 29 "Come, see a man who told me everything that I have done. Can this be the Christ?" 30 They went out of the city, and were coming to him.

31 In the meanwhile, the disciples urged him, saying, "Rabbi, eat."

32 But he said to them, "I have food to eat that you don't know about."

33 The disciples therefore said to one another, "Has anyone brought him something to eat?"

34 Jesus said to them, "My food is to do the will of him who sent me and to accomplish his work. 35 Don't you say, 'There are yet four months until the harvest?' Behold, I tell you, lift up your eyes and look at the fields, that they are white for harvest already. 36 He who reaps receives wages and gathers fruit to eternal life, that both he who sows and he who reaps may rejoice together. 37 For in this the saying is true, 'One sows, and another reaps.' 38 I sent you to reap that for which you haven't labored. Others have labored, and you have entered into their labor."

39 From that city many of the Samaritans believed in him because of the word of the woman, who testified, "He told me everything that I have done." 40 So when the Samaritans came to him, they begged him to stay with them. He stayed there two days. 41 Many more believed because of his word. 42 They said to the woman, "Now we believe, not because of your speaking; for we have heard for ourselves, and know that this is indeed the Christ, the Savior of the world."

Notes

1. In journeying between Galilee and Judea, it was necessary to pass through Samaria, unless a detour was made by the Jordan.
2. A rabbi rarely spoke with a woman in public, and the Jews thought the Samaritans were outcasts.
3. A prophet was generally considered a person who could settle religious differences.
4. There was a Samaritan temple on Mount Gerizim.

Questions for Reflection, Prayer, and Discussion

1. Why might we think the woman was frightened when she realized that He had intimate knowledge of her life?

2. What was the turning point [if any] for this woman, when she seemed to realize that Jesus was possibly the promised Messiah?

3. What reasons may we have for thinking that this Samaritan is experienced the holiness of Jesus?

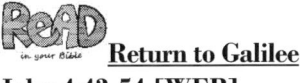 **Return to Galilee**
John 4:43-54 [WEB]
43 After the two days he went out from there and went into Galilee. 44 For Jesus himself testified that a prophet has no honor in his own country. 45 So when he came into Galilee, the Galileans received him, having seen all the things that he did in Jerusalem at the feast, for they also went to the feast. 46 Jesus came therefore again to Cana of Galilee, where he made the water into wine. There was a certain nobleman whose son was sick at Capernaum. 47 When he heard that Jesus had come out of Judea into Galilee, he went to him and begged him that he would come down and heal his son, for he was at the point of death. 48 Jesus therefore said to him, "Unless you see signs and wonders, you will in no way believe."

49 The nobleman said to him, "Sir, come down before my child dies."

50 Jesus said to him, "Go your way. Your son lives." The man believed the word that Jesus spoke to him, and he went his way. 51 As he was going down, his servants met him and reported, saying "Your child lives!" 52 So he inquired of them the hour when he began to get better. They said therefore to him, "Yesterday at the seventh hour, the fever left him." 53 So the father knew that it was at that hour in which Jesus said to him, "Your son lives." He believed, as did his whole house. 54 This is again the second sign that Jesus did, having come out of Judea into Galilee.

Notes
1. The Royal Official suggests someone from King Herod's house.
2. When Jesus speaks of signs and wonders [48], the Greek grammar has **you** in the plural, that is, it is addressed to the whole group.

Questions for Reflection, Prayer, and Discussion
1. Why do you suppose that a ***prophet*** [44] ***has no honor?***

2. Since this is the second sign, what was the first?

3. Can growth towards holiness bring about the glorification of God in this person?

Chapter Five
Holiness Heals

ReAD in your Bible **An Encounter and Illegal Gift of Grace**
John 5:1-18 [WEB]

1 After these things, there was a feast of the Jews, and Jesus went up to Jerusalem. 2 Now in Jerusalem by the sheep gate, there is a pool, which is called in Hebrew, "Bethesda", having five porches. 3 In these lay a great multitude of those who were sick, blind, lame, or paralyzed, waiting for the moving of the water; 4 for an angel went down at certain times into the pool and stirred up the water. Whoever stepped in first after the stirring of the water was healed of whatever disease he had. 5 A certain man was there who had been sick for thirty-eight years. 6 When Jesus saw him lying there, and knew that he had been sick for a long time, he asked him, "Do you want to be made well?"

7 The sick man answered him, "Sir, I have no one to put me into the pool when the water is stirred up, but while I'm coming, another steps down before me."

8 Jesus said to him, "Arise, take up your mat, and walk."

9 Immediately, the man was made well, and took up his mat and walked.

Now that day was a Sabbath. 10 So the Jews said to him who was cured, "It is the Sabbath. It is not lawful for you to carry the mat."

11 He answered them, "He who made me well said to me, 'Take up your mat and walk.'"

12 Then they asked him, "Who is the man who said to you, 'Take up your mat and walk'?"

13 But he who was healed didn't know who it was, for Jesus had withdrawn, a crowd being in the place.

14 Afterward Jesus found him in the temple and said to him, "Behold, you are made well. Sin no more, so that nothing worse happens to you."

15 The man went away, and told the Jews that it was Jesus who had made him well. 16 For this cause the Jews persecuted Jesus and sought to kill him, because he did these things on the Sabbath. 17 But Jesus answered them, "My Father is still working, so I am working, too." 18 For this cause therefore the Jews sought all the more to kill him, because he not only broke the Sabbath, but also called God his own Father, making himself equal with God.

Notes

1. References to Jews in John are not examples of antisemitism – John was Jewish. Rather, they refer to the authorities of the Jewish Temple, who felt threatened by the popularity of Jesus.
2. Chronologically, this probably takes place during the Festival of Booths, which remembers their years of wandering in the wilderness in tents.
3. Jesus asks the question because the man may have become accustomed to receiving alms and sympathy and may have long since given up on being healed.

Questions for Reflection, Prayer, and Discussion

1. Do you live as well as pray in Jesus' name?

2. Do you think Jesus had the same compassion for those who were His critics as those who were healed?

3. How might experiencing Jesus' holiness through healing have affected this man beyond his healing?

ReAD in your Bible **Jesus' Most Vital Relationship**
John 5:19-29 [WEB]

19 Jesus therefore answered them, "Most certainly, I tell you, the Son can do nothing of himself, but what he sees the Father doing. For whatever things he does, these the Son also does likewise. 20 For the Father has affection for the Son, and shows him all things that he himself does. He will show him greater works than these, that you may marvel. 21 For as the Father raises the dead and gives them life, even so the Son also gives life to whom he desires. 22 For the Father judges no one, but he has given all judgment to the Son, 23 that all may honor the Son, even as they honor the Father. He who doesn't honor the Son doesn't honor the Father who sent him.

24 "Most certainly I tell you, he who hears my word and believes him who sent me has eternal life, and doesn't come into judgment, but has passed out of death into life. 25 Most certainly I tell you, the hour comes, and now is, when the dead will hear the Son of God's voice; and those who hear will live. 26 For as the Father has life in himself, even so he gave to the Son also to have life in himself. 27 He also gave him authority to execute judgment, because he is a son of man. 28 Don't marvel at this, for the hour comes in which all who are in the tombs will hear his voice 29 and will come out; those who have done good, to the resurrection of life; and those who have done evil, to the resurrection of judgment.

Notes

1. Once again, Jesus reveals a portion of His interior life through John. The relationship of Jesus to God is in terms of correspondence of His will and activities with the will and activities of God.
2. When a person listens in faith, it gives a new life to a spiritually dead person.

Questions for Reflection, Prayer, and Discussion

1. When you pray, how easy for you is it to surrender to God's will in an honest and complete way?

2. When Jesus talks about His being *one* with God, do you find it easier to have that kind of relationship with Him?

3. Describe any desire you may have to be close to God through Jesus.

ReAD Documenting Jesus' Sonship
John 5:30-40 [WEB]

30 I can of myself do nothing. As I hear, I judge; and my judgment is righteous, because I don't seek my own will, but the will of my Father who sent me.

31 "If I testify about myself, my witness is not valid. 32 It is another who testifies about me. I know that the testimony which he testifies about me is true. 33 You have sent to John, and he has testified to the truth. 34 But the testimony which I receive is not from man. However, I say these things that you may be saved. 35 He was the burning and shining lamp, and you were willing to rejoice for a while in his light. 36 But the testimony which I have is greater than that of John; for the works which the Father gave me to accomplish, the very works that I do, testify about me, that the Father has sent me. 37 The Father himself, who sent me, has testified about me. You have neither heard his voice at any time, nor seen his form. 38 You don't have his word living in you, because you don't believe him whom he sent.

39 "You search the Scriptures, because you think that in them you have eternal life; and these are they which testify about me. 40 Yet you will not come to me, that you may have life.

Notes
1. The actions and teachings of Jesus reflect his inward life with God, and they help to establish the divine connection. It is therefore part of His character to be righteous before God.
2. We are right when our actions carry out our relationships. Justice is the fulfillment of righteousness, which in turn fulfills relationships.
3. The **search** [39] can be translated either as a reflection of what has already been done or as a command to verify what it says.

Questions for Reflection, Prayer, and Discussion
1. If you do something that is unrighteous or sinful, how does that affect your being a faithful Christian?

2. How would you describe the importance for you to have a good relationship with Jesus as your Savior?

3. What can you do to make a conscious effort to try to be like Jesus in terms of His character?

ReAD in your Bible **The Consequences of Rejection**
John 5:41-47 [WEB]

41 I don't receive glory from men. 42 But I know you, that you don't have God's love in yourselves. 43 I have come in my Father's name, and you don't receive me. If another comes in his own name, you will receive him. 44 How can you believe, who receive glory from one another, and you don't seek the glory that comes from the only God?

45 "Don't think that I will accuse you to the Father. There is one who accuses you, even Moses, on whom you have set your hope. 46 For if you believed Moses, you would believe me; for he wrote about me. 47 But if you don't believe his writings, how will you believe my words?"

Notes

1. Jesus does not live by human norms, but by those of God.
2. Human judgement has its roots in pride rather than in the love of God.
3. The standard-bearer of the rulers of the Temple, Moses, provides the basis of judgment against them.

Questions for Reflection, Prayer, and Discussion
1. How is being 'good' – based upon the law – different from fulfilling your relationship with Jesus?

2. What is your relationship to the law once you have accepted Jesus as your Savior and start following Him?

3. When following Jesus, do you try to see other people as Jesus does?

Chapter Six
Holiness Provides

ReAD in your Bible **Feeding Five Thousand Men plus Women, Children, and Slaves**

John 6:1-15 [WEB]

1 Jesus could not let them turn Him into a political messiah – the Devil had previously tempted Him with it. 6 After these things, Jesus went away to the other side of the sea of Galilee, which is also called the Sea of Tiberias. 2 A great multitude followed him, because they saw his signs which he did on those who were sick. 3 Jesus went up into the mountain, and he sat there with his disciples. 4 Now the Passover, the feast of the Jews, was at hand. 5 Jesus therefore, lifting up his eyes and seeing that a great multitude was coming to him, said to Philip, "Where are we to buy bread, that these may eat?" 6 He said this to test him, for he himself knew what he would do.

7 Philip answered him, "Two hundred denarii worth of bread is not sufficient for them, that every one of them may receive a little."

8 One of his disciples, Andrew, Simon Peter's brother, said to him, 9 "There is a boy here who has five barley loaves and two fish, but what are these among so many?"

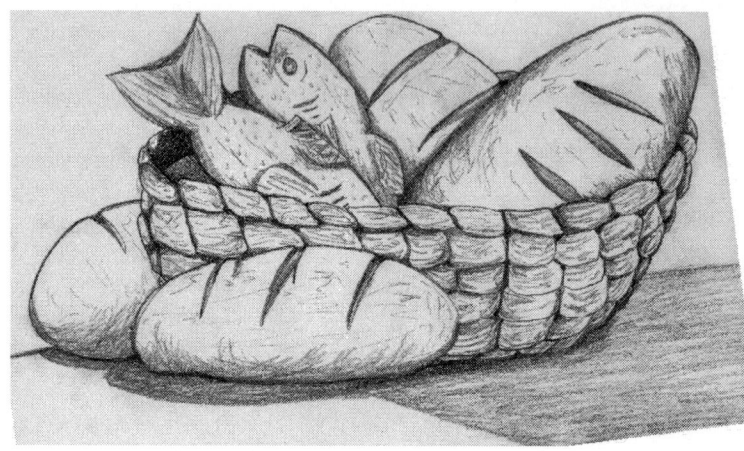

10 Jesus said, "Have the people sit down." Now there was much grass in that place. So the men sat down, in number about five thousand. 11 Jesus took the loaves, and having given thanks, he distributed to the disciples, and the disciples to those who were sitting down, likewise also of the fish as much as they desired. 12 When they were filled, he said to his disciples, "Gather up the broken pieces which are left over, that nothing be lost." 13 So they gathered them up, and filled twelve baskets with broken pieces from the five barley loaves, which were left over by those who had eaten. 14 When therefore the people saw the sign which Jesus did, they said, "This is truly the prophet who comes into the world." 15 Jesus therefore, perceiving that they were about to come and take him by force to make him king, withdrew again to the mountain by himself.

Notes
1. This is the only miracle recorded in all four Gospels.
2. Barley loaves were the principal staple of the poor, often cooked on hot rocks in the sun.
3. The remains were collected in twelve baskets – possibly one basket for each in the inner circle of twelve.

Questions for Reflection, Prayer, and Discussion
1. What kinds of hunger were present among those in the crowd besides hunger for food?

2. Besides satisfying physical hunger, what may have changed that day, if anything, for some of the people in the crowd?

3. If you were in that crowd, what are some of the impressions you might have had of Jesus?

READ Encounter on the Sea of Galilee
John 6:16-21 [WEB]

16 When evening came, his disciples went down to the sea. 17 They entered into the boat, and were going over the sea to Capernaum. It was now dark, and Jesus had not come to them. 18 The sea was tossed by a great wind blowing. 19 When therefore they had rowed about twenty-five or thirty stadia, they saw Jesus walking on the sea and drawing near to the boat; and they were afraid. 20 But he said to them, "It is I. Don't be afraid." 21 They were willing therefore to receive him into the boat. Immediately the boat was at the land where they were going.

Notes
1. This account attests that Jesus' authority is more than merely spiritual or political.
2. Jesus provides a larger understanding of who He was and a physical illustration of His holiness.

Questions for Reflection, Prayer, and Discussion
1. What are the primary lessons in this story?

2. Why were they afraid of when they saw Jesus?

3. Picturing yourself in the boat with the disciples, what impressions do you have of Jesus?

READ: The Crowds Want More of Jesus
John 6:22-24 [WEB]

22 On the next day, the multitude that stood on the other side of the sea saw that there was no other boat there, except the one in which his disciples had embarked, and that Jesus hadn't entered with his disciples into the boat, but his disciples had gone away alone. 23 However, boats from Tiberias came near to the place where they ate the bread after the Lord had given thanks. 24 When the multitude therefore saw that Jesus wasn't there, nor his disciples, they themselves got into the boats and came to Capernaum, seeking Jesus.

Note

With their physical hunger satisfied, they did not recognize the miracle for what it was.

Questions for Reflection, Prayer, and Discussion

1. Why do you think most of the crowd probably failed to recognize what had happened at the meal?

2. Have you constructed your own faith in God, or is God the source of the growth of your faith?

READ: Jesus Is the Bread of Life
John 6:25-59 [WEB]

25 When they found him on the other side of the sea, they asked him, "Rabbi, when did you come here?"

26 Jesus answered them, "Most certainly I tell you, you seek me, not because you saw signs, but because you ate of the loaves and were filled. 27 Don't work for the food which perishes, but for the food which remains to eternal life, which the Son of Man will give to you. For God the Father has sealed him."

28 They said therefore to him, "What must we do, that we may work the works of God?"

29 Jesus answered them, "This is the work of God, that you believe in him whom he has sent."

30 They said therefore to him, "What then do you do for a sign, that we may see and believe you? What work do you do? 31 Our fathers ate the manna in the wilderness. As it is written, 'He gave them bread out of heaven to eat.' "

32 Jesus therefore said to them, "Most certainly, I tell you, it wasn't Moses who gave you the bread out of heaven, but my Father gives you the true bread out of heaven. 33 For the bread of God is that which comes down out of heaven and gives life to the world."

34 They said therefore to him, "Lord, always give us this bread."

35 Jesus said to them, "I am the bread of life. Whoever comes to me will not be hungry, and whoever believes in me will never be thirsty. 36 But I told you that you have seen me, and yet you don't believe. 37 All those whom the Father gives me will come to me. He who comes to me I will in no way throw out. 38 For I have come down from heaven, not to do my own will, but the will of him who sent me. 39 This is the will of my Father who sent me, that of all he has given to me I should lose nothing, but should raise him up at the last day. 40 This is the will of the one who sent me, that everyone who sees the Son and believes in him should have eternal life; and I will raise him up at the last day."

41 The Jews therefore murmured concerning him, because he said, "I am the bread which came down out of heaven." 42 They said, "Isn't this Jesus, the son of Joseph, whose father and mother we know? How then does he say, 'I have come down out of heaven?' "

43 Therefore Jesus answered them, "Don't murmur among yourselves. 44 No one can come to me unless the Father who sent me draws him; and I will raise him up in the last day. 45 It is written in the prophets, 'They will all be taught by God.' Therefore everyone who hears from the Father and has learned, comes to me. 46 Not that anyone has seen the Father, except he who is from God. He has seen the Father. 47 Most certainly, I tell you, he who believes in me has eternal life. 48 I am the bread of life. 49 Your fathers ate the manna in the wilderness and they died. 50 This is the bread which comes down out of heaven, that anyone may eat of it and not die. 51 I am the living bread which came down out of heaven. If anyone eats of this bread, he will live forever. Yes, the bread which I will give for the life of the world is my flesh."

52 The Jews therefore contended with one another, saying, "How can this man give us his flesh to eat?"

53 Jesus therefore said to them, "Most certainly I tell you, unless you eat the flesh of the Son of Man and drink his blood, you don't have life in yourselves. 54 He who eats my flesh and drinks my blood has eternal life, and I will raise him up at the last day. 55 For my flesh is food indeed, and my blood is drink indeed. 56 He who eats my flesh and drinks my blood lives in me, and I in him. 57 As the living Father sent me, and I live because of the Father, so he who feeds on me will also live because of me. 58 This is the bread which came down out of heaven—not as our fathers ate the manna and died. He who eats this bread will live forever." 59 He said these things in the synagogue, as he taught in Capernaum.

Notes

1. The seal [27] was perhaps the descent of the Holy Spirit as a dove when He was baptized.
2. The bread of which Jesus speaks is vitally important in John's testimony to Christians. As the Gospel of John unfolds, it uses the teachings of Christ on bread as a recurrent theme.
3. John does not remind us of what Jesus said about the bread and wine in his account of the Last Supper. Instead, John reminds his readers of Jesus' teachings about His flesh and Blood. [53-58]

Questions for Reflection, Prayer, and Discussion

1. How does eating the bread make you a part of Jesus – and makes Jesus a part of you – when you share in the Lord's Supper?

2. How does drinking the cup affect you as a sinner?

3. Does sharing in the Lord's Supper help grow your faith and your growth towards holiness?

Many of Jesus' Followers Desert Him
John 6:60-71 [WEB]

60 Therefore many of his disciples, when they heard this, said, "This is a hard saying! Who can listen to it?"

61 But Jesus knowing in himself that his disciples murmured at this, said to them, "Does this cause you to stumble? 62 Then what if you would see the Son of Man ascending to where he was before? 63 It is the spirit who gives life. The flesh profits nothing. The words that I speak to you are spirit, and are life. 64 But there are some of you who don't believe." For Jesus knew from the beginning who they were who didn't believe, and who it was who would betray him. 65 He said, "For this cause I have said to you that no one can come to me, unless it is given to him by my Father."

66 At this, many of his disciples went back and walked no more with him. 67 Jesus said therefore to the twelve, "You don't also want to go away, do you?"

68 Simon Peter answered him, "Lord, to whom would we go? You have the words of eternal life. 69 We have come to believe and know that you are the Christ, the Son of the living God."

70 Jesus answered them, "Didn't I choose you, the twelve, and one of you is a devil?" 71 Now he spoke of Judas, the son of Simon Iscariot, for it was he who would betray him, being one of the twelve.

Notes
1. This teaching emphasizes the complete union between Jesus and his disciples at the table of the Lord. John marks this as a turning point – after which many of His followers begin to fall away.
2. After the confession of Peter, John refers to Judas for the first time in his gospel.

A Question for Reflection, Prayer, and Discussion

What are some ways that some of Jesus' followers today betray Him?

Chapter Seven
Holiness Is Distinctive

READ **Staying Behind in Galilee**
John 7:1-10 [WEB]

After these things, Jesus was walking in Galilee, for he wouldn't walk in Judea, because the Jews sought to kill him. 2 Now the feast of the Jews, the Feast of Booths, was at hand. 3 His brothers therefore said to him, "Depart from here and go into Judea, that your disciples also may see your works which you do. 4 For no one does anything in secret while he seeks to be known openly. If you do these things, reveal yourself to the world." 5 For even his brothers didn't believe in him.

6 Jesus therefore said to them, "My time has not yet come, but your time is always ready. 7 The world can't hate you, but it hates me, because I testify about it, that its works are evil. 8 You go up to the feast. I am not yet going up to this feast, because my time is not yet fulfilled."

9 Having said these things to them, he stayed in Galilee. 10 But when his brothers had gone up to the feast, then he also went up, not publicly, but as it were in secret.

Notes

1. It is early fall. The followers of Jesus go to Jerusalem for an annual feast (Sukkot) to remember the wanderings of their people in the desert before entering the Promised Land and for the autumn harvest.
2. Jesus' brothers want him to verify his claims to Messiahship in Jerusalem. Once again, Jesus verifies that his program is not his own or theirs, but God's.

Questions for Reflection, Prayer, and Discussion

1. Do you think Jesus wants time alone to evaluate His progress and to spend time in prayer, or might he have other motives for staying behind?

2. What part of Jesus' character do you see revealed here, when He lets His close friends travel on to Jerusalem?

3. How could He help His disciples grow spiritually by doing this?

 **A Secret Arrival**
John 7:11-13 [WEB]

11 The Jews therefore sought him at the feast, and said, "Where is he?" 12 There was much murmuring among the multitudes concerning him. Some said, "He is a good man." Others said, "Not so, but he leads the multitude astray." 13 Yet no one spoke openly of him for fear of the Jews.

Notes

1. The fear of the authorities of the Jewish Temple feeds the debate between the twelve about the character of Jesus.
2. Most rabbis would identify the teacher they learned from as the source of their authority.

Questions for Reflection, Prayer, and Discussion

1. What motive do you see for Jesus' letting his followers travel on ahead?

2. What emotions can you see in the fully human Jesus at this point in His earthly ministry?

Public Disclosure and Teaching
John 7:14-24 [WEB]

14 But when it was now the middle of the feast, Jesus went up into the temple and taught. 15 The Jews therefore marveled, saying, "How does this man know letters, having never been educated?"

16 Jesus therefore answered them, "My teaching is not mine, but his who sent me. 17 If anyone desires to do his will, he will know about the teaching, whether it is from God or if I am speaking from myself. 18 He who speaks from himself seeks his own glory, but he who seeks the glory of him who sent him is true, and no unrighteousness is in him. 19 Didn't Moses give you the law, and yet none of you keeps the law? Why do you seek to kill me?"

20 The multitude answered, "You have a demon! Who seeks to kill you?"

21 Jesus answered them, "I did one work and you all marvel because of it. 22 Moses has given you circumcision (not that it is of Moses, but of the fathers), and on the Sabbath you circumcise a boy. 23 If a boy receives circumcision on the Sabbath, that the law of Moses may not be broken, are you angry with me because I made a man completely healthy on the Sabbath? 24 Don't judge according to appearance, but judge righteous judgment."

Notes

1. The will of God, instead of the teachings of one rabbi, is the authority of his teaching.
2. The Torah forbids a person to be executed for healing on the Sabbath. Leviticus 12 allows circumcision on the Sabbath, so logically healing would also be allowed.
3. As we faithfully follow Jesus and try to become like Him, we can easily experience negative reactions as Jesus did, even from people who claim to be Christian.

Questions for Reflection, Prayer, and Discussion

1. Describe any authority Jesus has in your life.

2. How do you observe a Sabbath day of rest each week, resting one day out of seven?

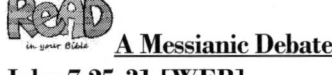 **A Messianic Debate**

John 7:25-31 [WEB]

25 Therefore some of them of Jerusalem said, "Isn't this he whom they seek to kill? 26 Behold, he speaks openly, and they say nothing to him. Can it be that the rulers indeed know that this is truly the Christ? 27 However, we know where this man comes from, but when the Christ comes, no one will know where he comes from."

28 Jesus therefore cried out in the temple, teaching and saying, "You both know me, and know where I am from. I have not come of myself, but he who sent me is true, whom you don't know. 29 I know him, because I am from him, and he sent me."

30 They sought therefore to take him; but no one laid a hand on him, because his hour had not yet come. 31 But of the multitude, many believed in him. They said, "When the Christ comes, he won't do more signs than those which this man has done, will he?"

Note

Traditionally, the earthly origin of the Messiah was believed to be a mystery, and Jesus was known to have grown up in Nazareth, hence the debate.

Questions for Reflection, Prayer, and Discussion

1. When you want to know someone's credentials, what kind of documentation do you seek?

2. What are some ways to verify someone's credentials when written records are not available?

3. Do you think there are people that can see holiness in you because you follow Jesus and try to be like Him, unlike others?

READ Enemies Unite
John 7:32-36 [WEB]

32 The Pharisees heard the multitude murmuring these things concerning him, and the chief priests and the Pharisees sent officers to arrest him.

33 Then Jesus said, "I will be with you a little while longer, then I go to him who sent me. 34 You will seek me and won't find me. You can't come where I am."

35 The Jews therefore said among themselves, "Where will this man go that we won't find him? Will he go to the Dispersion among the Greeks and teach the Greeks? 36 What is this word that he said, 'You will seek me, and won't find me;' and 'Where I am, you can't come'?"

Note
The chief priests during this period are evidently Sadducees, who are ecclesiastical enemies of the Pharisees.

Questions for Reflection, Prayer, and Discussion

1. What are the reasons that the leaders of the religious establishment are so anxious to get rid of Jesus?

2. Why do the temple leaders not get the point, that in heaven, He will be beyond their reach?

Read Festival Highlight
John 7:37-44 [WEB]

37 Now on the last and greatest day of the feast, Jesus stood and cried out, "If anyone is thirsty, let him come to me and drink! 38 He who believes in me, as the Scripture has said, from within him will flow rivers of living water." 39 But he said this about the Spirit, which those believing in him were to receive. For the Holy Spirit was not yet given, because Jesus wasn't yet glorified.

40 Many of the multitude therefore, when they heard these words, said, "This is truly the prophet." 41 Others said, "This is the Christ." But some said, "What, does the Christ come out of Galilee? 42 Hasn't the Scripture said that the Christ comes of the offspring of David, and from Bethlehem, the village where David was?" 43 So a division arose in the multitude because of him. 44 Some of them would have arrested him, but no one laid hands on him.

Notes

1. During the festival, for seven days, water was brought from the pool of Siloam to the Temple in memory of the water of the rock in the desert [Numbers 20]. It is a symbol of the expectation of deliverance through the Messiah.
2. In Jesus, the water symbolizing the rock in the wilderness becomes the reality of the coming of the Messiah.
3. Once again, the issue is the geographic origin of the messiah.

Questions for Reflection, Prayer, and Discussion

1. How do you react to Jesus when He describes Himself as living water?

2. Why do you think John may have thought that this dialogue was important in his testimony?

READ: The Police Seek Justice
John 7:45-52 [WEB]

45 The officers therefore came to the chief priests and Pharisees; and they said to them, "Why didn't you bring him?"

46 The officers answered, "No man ever spoke like this man!"

47 The Pharisees therefore answered them, "You aren't also led astray, are you? 48 Have any of the rulers or any of the Pharisees believed in him? 49 But this multitude that doesn't know the law is cursed."

50 Nicodemus (he who came to him by night, being one of them) said to them, 51 "Does our law judge a man unless it first hears from him personally and knows what he does?"

52 They answered him, "Are you also from Galilee? Search and see that no prophet has arisen out of Galilee."

Notes

1. The authorities of Jerusalem show contempt for the Galilean peasantry. [52]
2. They focus on issues that are otherwise unimportant. It is the second appearing of Nicodemus in the testimony of John.

Questions for Reflection, Prayer, and Discussion

1. Was Nicodemus really defending Jesus or seeking logic for their arguments?

2. What was the role of pride in this debate?

Questions for Further Reflection and Discussion

The twelve apostles have been with Jesus for many months now. They have been living with Him and are getting to know Him. Consider how their spiritual lives have changed and how that change has affected their behavior. Consider how Jesus' inner circle is beginning to reflect the holiness of Jesus. Think about the changes you see in them in light of your own journey of faith. If you can identify any changes you see in the twelve apostles, write them down.

As pushing ahead on the path of prayer and holiness is a prime form of spiritual warfare against sin and Satan, so it is an educational process that God has planned and programmed in order to refine, purge, enlarge, animate, toughen, and mature us. By means of it He brings us progressively into the moral and spiritual shape in which He wants to see us.

Packer, J. I.. *Rediscovering Holiness* (p. 15). Baker Publishing Group. Kindle Edition.

Chapter Eight
Holiness Has Authority

A Test of Authority
John 7:53-8:11 [WEB]

7:53 Everyone went to his own house, 8:1 but Jesus went to the Mount of Olives.

2 Now very early in the morning, he came again into the temple, and all the people came to him. He sat down and taught them. 3 The scribes and the Pharisees brought a woman taken in adultery. Having set her in the middle, 4 they told him, "Teacher, we found this woman in adultery, in the very act. 5 Now in our law, Moses commanded us to stone such women. What then do you say about her?" 6 They said this testing him, that they might have something to accuse him of.

But Jesus stooped down and wrote on the ground with his finger. 7 But when they continued asking him, he looked up and said to them, "He who is without sin among you, let him throw the first stone at her." 8 Again he stooped down and wrote on the ground with his finger.

9 They, when they heard it, being convicted by their conscience, went out one by one, beginning from the oldest, even to the last. Jesus was left alone with the woman where she was, in the middle. 10 Jesus, standing up, saw her and said, "Woman, where are your accusers? Did no one condemn you?"

11 She said, "No one, Lord."

Jesus said, "Neither do I condemn you. Go your way. From now on, sin no more."

Notes

1. Sinless in this case would be the innocent or wounded party in this alleged case of adultery.
2. The snare was in Jesus not having been presented with two witnesses agreeing [Deuteronomy 19:15] on the charges against the woman. If Jesus pronounced his judgment without hearing two or more matching witnesses, He would violate the Torah.
3. Jesus' looking down rather than toward her during the turmoil was an act of profound respect. She had possibly been stripped of her garments.

Questions for Reflection, Prayer, and Discussion

1. Describe a time when you have been tempted to go with the flow of the emotions of the moment rather than to act with sound judgment.

2. Why might the Temple leaders take the risk presenting this case without valid witnesses?

3. If you see Jesus' holiness in this passage, describe it and what it means to you.

Read Jesus is the Light
John 8:12-20 [WEB]

12 Again, therefore, Jesus spoke to them, saying, "I am the light of the world. He who follows me will not walk in the darkness, but will have the light of life."

13 The Pharisees therefore said to him, "You testify about yourself. Your testimony is not valid."

14 Jesus answered them, "Even if I testify about myself, my testimony is true, for I know where I came from, and where I am going; but you don't know where I came from, or where I am going. 15 You judge according to the flesh. I judge no one. 16 Even if I do judge, my judgment is true, for I am not alone, but I am with the Father who sent me. 17 It's also written in your law that the testimony of two people is valid. 18 I am one who testifies about myself, and the Father who sent me testifies about me."

19 They said therefore to him, "Where is your Father?"

Jesus answered, "You know neither me nor my Father. If you knew me, you would know my Father also." 20 Jesus spoke these words in the treasury, as he taught in the temple. Yet no one arrested him, because his hour had not yet come.

Notes

1. Large golden lamps adorned the Temple during the Feast of Tabernacles, and Jesus evidently took the occasion to reinforce His claim to the light of the world.
2. The heavenly origin of Jesus implies that on earth He alone comprehends perfectly who He is.

Questions for Reflection, Prayer, and Discussion

1. Describe an experience where your being a follower of Christ has helped you understand the world better?

2. Describe how Christ's life and teachings enlighten your ability to cope with life?

READ Forecast of His Passion
John 8:21-30 [WEB]

21 Jesus said therefore again to them, "I am going away, and you will seek me, and you will die in your sins. Where I go, you can't come."

22 The Jews therefore said, "Will he kill himself, because he says, 'Where I am going, you can't come'?"

23 He said to them, "You are from beneath. I am from above. You are of this world. I am not of this world. 24 I said therefore to you that you will die in your sins; for unless you believe that I am he, you will die in your sins."

25 They said therefore to him, "Who are you?"

Jesus said to them, "Just what I have been saying to you from the beginning. 26 I have many things to speak and to judge concerning you. However, he who sent me is true; and the things which I heard from him, these I say to the world."

27 They didn't understand that he spoke to them about the Father. 28 Jesus therefore said to them, "When you have lifted up the Son of Man, then you will know that I am he, and I do nothing of myself, but as my Father taught me, I say these things. 29 He who sent me is with me. The Father hasn't left me alone, for I always do the things that are pleasing to him."

30 As he spoke these things, many believed in him.

Note

They supposed that he was referring to suicide, because it was believed in this culture to separate one from God and his relatives forever.

Questions for Reflection, Prayer, and Discussion

1. Why do you suppose he told them they would die in their sin (singular) [21] rather than die in their sins?

2. When Jesus says that He has much to condemn [26], how does that put Him in the role of judge?

3. Why did they not understand that He was talking about God [27]?

Read: The Formula for True Freedom
John 8:31-47 [WEB]

31 Jesus therefore said to those Jews who had believed him, "If you remain in my word, then you are truly my disciples. 32 You will know the truth, and the truth will make you free."

33 They answered him, "We are Abraham's offspring, and have never been in bondage to anyone. How do you say, 'You will be made free'?"

34 Jesus answered them, "Most certainly I tell you, everyone who commits sin is the bondservant of sin. 35 A bondservant doesn't live in the house forever. A son remains forever. 36 If therefore the Son makes you free, you will be free indeed. 37 I know that you are Abraham's offspring, yet you seek to kill me, because my word finds no place in you. 38 I say the things which I have seen with my Father; and you also do the things which you have seen with your father."

39 They answered him, "Our father is Abraham."

Jesus said to them, "If you were Abraham's children, you would do the works of Abraham. 40 But now you seek to kill me, a man who has told you the truth which I heard from God. Abraham didn't do this. 41 You do the works of your father."

They said to him, "We were not born of sexual immorality. We have one Father, God."

42 Therefore Jesus said to them, "If God were your father, you would love me, for I came out and have come from God. For I haven't come of myself, but he sent me. 43 Why don't you understand my speech? Because you can't hear my word. 44 You are of your father the devil, and you want to do the desires of your father. He was a murderer from the beginning, and doesn't stand in the truth, because there is no truth in him. When he speaks a lie, he speaks on his own; for he is a liar, and the father of lies. 45 But because I tell the truth, you don't believe me. 46 Which of you convicts me of sin? If I tell the truth, why do you not believe me? 47 He who is of God hears the words of God. For this cause you don't hear, because you are not of God."

Notes
1. Liberty here means being liberated from the power of sin, which enslaves us to our past and inhibits our future.
2. Their desire to kill Jesus severs them under the law of their right to inherit as descendants of Abraham.

Questions for Reflection, Prayer, and Discussion
1. Describe how we tend to be held down by the sins of our pasts.

2. What do you think is the best way to let go of the past and then claim the future with Christ?

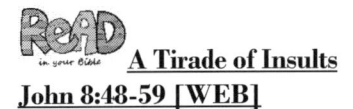

Read: A Tirade of Insults
John 8:48-59 [WEB]

48 Then the Jews answered him, "Don't we say well that you are a Samaritan, and have a demon?"

49 Jesus answered, "I don't have a demon, but I honor my Father and you dishonor me. 50 But I don't seek my own glory. There is one who seeks and judges. 51 Most certainly, I tell you, if a person keeps my word, he will never see death."

52 Then the Jews said to him, "Now we know that you have a demon. Abraham died, as did the prophets; and you say, 'If a man keeps my word, he will never taste of death.' 53 Are you greater than our father Abraham, who died? The prophets died. Who do you make yourself out to be?"

54 Jesus answered, "If I glorify myself, my glory is nothing. It is my Father who glorifies me, of whom you say that he is our God. 55 You have not known him, but I know him. If I said, 'I don't know him,' I would be like you, a liar. But I know him and keep his word. 56 Your father Abraham rejoiced to see my day. He saw it and was glad."

57 The Jews therefore said to him, "You are not yet fifty years old! Have you seen Abraham?"

58 Jesus said to them, "Most certainly, I tell you, before Abraham came into existence, I AM."

59 Therefore they took up stones to throw at him, but Jesus hid himself and went out of the temple, having gone through the middle of them, and so passed by.

Notes
1. Since evil often disguises itself as good, they now claim that the miracles associated with Jesus are deceiving deeds of evil.
2. Since the current Temple leaders are Sadducees who do not believe in the resurrection or the afterlife, they cannot accept Jesus' teachings about death and life.

Questions for Reflection, Prayer, and Discussion
1. How is Jesus dishonored by their accusations?

2. How would they have better understood what He was teaching if they believed in resurrection?

3. If you have a hunger to be more like Jesus and not merely follow Him, describe it.

Chapter Nine
Holiness Brings Wisdom

READ **A Blind Man's Healing**
John 9:1-12 [WEB]

1 As he passed by, he saw a man blind from birth. 2 His disciples asked him, "Rabbi, who sinned, this man or his parents, that he was born blind?"

3 Jesus answered, "This man didn't sin, nor did his parents, but that the works of God might be revealed in him. 4 I must work the works of him who sent me while it is day. The night is coming, when no one can work. 5 While I am in the world, I am the light of the world." 6 When he had said this, he spat on the ground, made mud with the saliva, anointed the blind man's eyes with the mud, 7 and said to him, "Go, wash in the pool of Siloam" (which means "Sent"). So he went away, washed, and came back seeing.

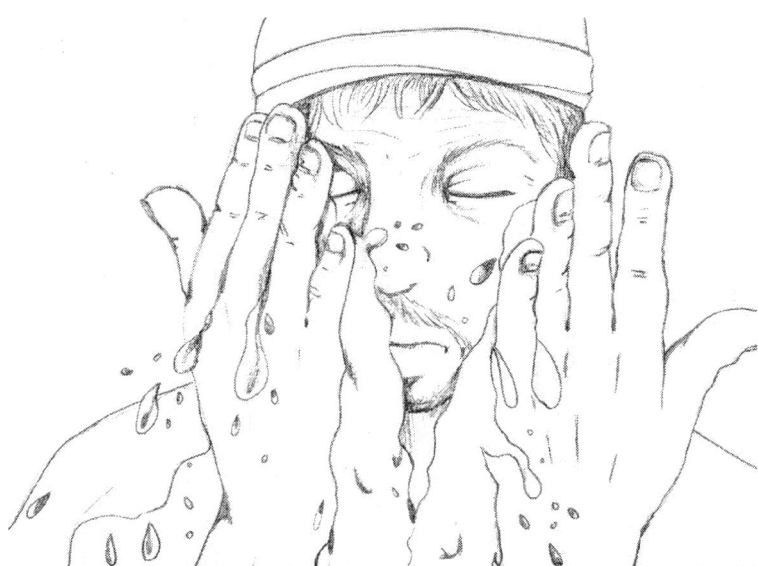

8 Therefore the neighbors and those who saw that he was blind before said, "Isn't this he who sat and begged?" 9 Others were saying, "It is he." Still others were saying, "He looks like him."

He said, "I am he."

10 They therefore were asking him, "How were your eyes opened?"

11 He answered, "A man called Jesus made mud, anointed my eyes, and said to me, 'Go to the pool of Siloam and wash.' So I went away and washed, and I received sight."

12 Then they asked him, "Where is he?"

He said, "I don't know."

Notes

1. A person's suffering was attributed to sin – by parents, by ancestors, or even by the child before he or she was born.
2. There was a belief that saliva had medicinal value. Also, making mud would be considered work – a violation of the Sabbath.

READ **The Pharisees Investigate the Healing**
John 9:13-34 [WEB]

13 They brought him who had been blind to the Pharisees. 14 It was a Sabbath when Jesus made the mud and opened his eyes. 15 Again therefore the Pharisees also asked him how he received his sight. He said to them, "He put mud on my eyes, I washed, and I see."

16 Some therefore of the Pharisees said, "This man is not from God, because he doesn't keep the Sabbath." Others said, "How can a man who is a sinner do such signs?" So there was division among them.

17 Therefore they asked the blind man again, "What do you say about him, because he opened your eyes?"

He said, "He is a prophet."

18 The Jews therefore didn't believe concerning him, that he had been blind and had received his sight, until they called the parents of him who had received his sight, 19 and asked them, "Is this your son, whom you say was born blind? How then does he now see?"

20 His parents answered them, "We know that this is our son, and that he was born blind; 21 but how he now sees, we don't know; or who opened his eyes, we don't know. He is of age. Ask him. He will speak for himself." 22 His parents said these things because they feared the Jews; for the Jews had already agreed that if any man would confess him as Christ, he would be put out of the synagogue. 23 Therefore his parents said, "He is of age. Ask him."

24 So they called the man who was blind a second time, and said to him, "Give glory to God. We know that this man is a sinner."

25 He therefore answered, "I don't know if he is a sinner. One thing I do know: that though I was blind, now I see."

26 They said to him again, "What did he do to you? How did he open your eyes?"

27 He answered them, "I told you already, and you didn't listen. Why do you want to hear it again? You don't also want to become his disciples, do you?"

28 They insulted him and said, "You are his disciple, but we are disciples of Moses. 29 We know that God has spoken to Moses. But as for this man, we don't know where he comes from."

30 The man answered them, "How amazing! You don't know where he comes from, yet he opened my eyes. 31 We know that God doesn't listen to sinners, but if anyone is a worshiper of God and does his will, he listens to him. 32 Since the world began it has never been heard of that anyone opened the eyes of someone born blind. 33 If this man were not from God, he could do nothing."

34 They answered him, "You were altogether born in sins, and do you teach us?" Then they threw him out.

<u>Notes</u>

1. Give glory to God was an idiomatic expression that commands the hearer to tell the truth.
2. The parents skillfully avoid participating in the controversy by letting their son enjoy his new status of fully functional adult.

<u>Questions for Reflection, Prayer, and Discussion</u>

1. If you have seen this phenomenon occur in church discussions, give an example.

2. Besides the man healed, who are the winners here?

3. As this man follows Jesus, why might we think he will become a faithful reflection of Jesus' holiness?

READ **Blindness of the Spirit**
John 9:35-41 [WEB]

35 Jesus heard that they had thrown him out, and finding him, he said, "Do you believe in the Son of God?"

36 He answered, "Who is he, Lord, that I may believe in him?"

37 Jesus said to him, "You have both seen him, and it is he who speaks with you."

38 He said, "Lord, I believe!" and he worshiped him.

39 Jesus said, "I came into this world for judgment, that those who don't see may see; and that those who see may become blind."

40 Those of the Pharisees who were with him heard these things, and said to him, "Are we also blind?"

41 Jesus said to them, "If you were blind, you would have no sin; but now you say, 'We see.' Therefore your sin remains."

Note

Jesus uses the man cured of his blindness as a teaching opportunity.

A Question for Reflection, Prayer, and Discussion

If you know anyone that you think may be spiritually blind, describe the blindness.

Chapter Ten
Jesus Is God's Holiness

READ in your Bible **Jesus the Shepherd**
John 10:1-18 [WEB]

1 "Most certainly, I tell you, one who doesn't enter by the door into the sheep fold, but climbs up some other way, is a thief and a robber. 2 But one who enters in by the door is the shepherd of the sheep. 3 The gatekeeper opens the gate for him, and the sheep listen to his voice. He calls his own sheep by name and leads them out. 4 Whenever he brings out his own sheep, he goes before them; and the sheep follow him, for they know his voice. 5 They will by no means follow a stranger, but will flee from him; for they don't know the voice of strangers." 6 Jesus spoke this parable to them, but they didn't understand what he was telling them.

7 Jesus therefore said to them again, "Most certainly, I tell you, I am the sheep's door. 8 All who came before me are thieves and robbers, but the sheep didn't listen to them. 9 I am the door. If anyone enters in by me, he will be saved, and will go in and go out and will find pasture. 10 The thief only comes to steal, kill, and destroy. I came that they may have life, and may have it abundantly.

11 "I am the good shepherd. The good shepherd lays down his life for the sheep. 12 He who is a hired hand, and not a shepherd, who doesn't own the sheep, sees the wolf coming, leaves the sheep, and flees. The wolf snatches the sheep and scatters them. 13 The hired hand flees because he is a hired hand and doesn't care for the sheep. 14 I am the good shepherd. I know my own, and I'm known by my own; 15 even as the Father knows me, and I know the Father. I lay down my life for the sheep. 16 I have other sheep which are not of this fold. I must bring them also, and they will hear my voice. They will become one flock with one shepherd. 17 Therefore the Father loves me, because I lay down my life, that I may take it again. 18 No one takes it away from me, but I lay it down by myself. I have power to lay it down, and I have power to take it again. I received this commandment from my Father."

Notes

1. A Gatekeeper was someone hired by several shepherds to take care of the sheep as one flock.
2. Jesus avoids the labels of allegory and metaphor by moving his allusions from the guard to the gate, and to the shepherd.

Questions for Reflection, Prayer, and Discussion

1. Since sheep are incredibly lacking in intelligence, how do you feel about being a sheep in Christ's flock?

2. Since it is easier to be a sheep than to be a shepherd, why are there not more people who want to be cared for by Jesus?

3. Does this passage indicate anything about the holiness of Jesus, and is it something you think you can reflect?

Continuing Controversy
John 10:19-21 [WEB]

19 Therefore a division arose again among the Jews because of these words. 20 Many of them said, "He has a demon and is insane! Why do you listen to him?" 21 Others said, "These are not the sayings of one possessed by a demon. It isn't possible for a demon to open the eyes of the blind, is it?"

Questions for Reflection, Prayer, and Discussion

1. Do you think a demon can open the eyes of the blind? Why do you think so?

2. What do you think should tilt the scales in Jesus' favor?

Read A Demand for Identity
John 10:22-30 [WEB]

22 It was the Feast of the Dedication at Jerusalem. 23 It was winter, and Jesus was walking in the temple, in Solomon's porch. 24 The Jews therefore came around him and said to him, "How long will you hold us in suspense? If you are the Christ, tell us plainly."

25 Jesus answered them, "I told you, and you don't believe. The works that I do in my Father's name, these testify about me. 26 But you don't believe, because you are not of my sheep, as I told you. 27 My sheep hear my voice, and I know them, and they follow me. 28 I give eternal life to them. They will never perish, and no one will snatch them out of my hand. 29 My Father who has given them to me is greater than all. No one is able to snatch them out of my Father's hand. 30 I and the Father are one."

Note

The Temple leaders wanted plain evidence of blasphemy.

Questions for Reflection, Prayer, and Discussion

1. Why do you think the rulers of the Temple don't understand who Jesus is?

2. Do Jesus' loving references to the Father add fuel to the fire?

3. Describe how His references to God as His father affect your faith.

Read in your Bible: Escape from False Judgment
John 10:31-42 [WEB]

31 Therefore the Jews took up stones again to stone him. 32 Jesus answered them, "I have shown you many good works from my Father. For which of those works do you stone me?"

33 The Jews answered him, "We don't stone you for a good work, but for blasphemy, because you, being a man, make yourself God."

34 Jesus answered them, "Isn't it written in your law, 'I said, you are gods?' 35 If he called them gods, to whom the word of God came (and the Scripture can't be broken), 36 do you say of him whom the Father sanctified and sent into the world, 'You blaspheme,' because I said, 'I am the Son of God?' 37 If I don't do the works of my Father, don't believe me. 38 But if I do them, though you don't believe me, believe the works, that you may know and believe that the Father is in me, and I in the Father."

39 They sought again to seize him, and he went out of their hand. 40 He went away again beyond the Jordan into the place where John was baptizing at first, and he stayed there. 41 Many came to him. They said, "John indeed did no sign, but everything that John said about this man is true." 42 Many believed in him there.

Notes
1. The situation becomes dangerous, and Jesus expands his defenses by claiming that actions are more important than titles.
2. Travelling to Perea, where his cousin John had worked, he found temporary relative security.

Questions for Reflection, Prayer, and Discussion
1. If you can, describe someone you know who works quietly for God's glory without seeking a chosen office, title, or recognition.

2. Do you believe that Jesus has pushed the Temple authorities too far in this instance?

Chapter Eleven
Holiness Fuels Life

The Death of Lazarus
John 11:1-16 [WEB]

1 Now a certain man was sick, Lazarus from Bethany, of the village of Mary and her sister, Martha. 2 It was that Mary who had anointed the Lord with ointment and wiped his feet with her hair, whose brother Lazarus was sick. 3 The sisters therefore sent to him, saying, "Lord, behold, he for whom you have great affection is sick."

4 But when Jesus heard it, he said, "This sickness is not to death, but for the glory of God, that God's Son may be glorified by it." 5 Now Jesus loved Martha, and her sister, and Lazarus. 6 When therefore he heard that he was sick, he stayed two days in the place where he was. 7 Then after this he said to the disciples, "Let's go into Judea again."

8 The disciples asked him, "Rabbi, the Jews were just trying to stone you. Are you going there again?"

9 Jesus answered, "Aren't there twelve hours of daylight? If a man walks in the day, he doesn't stumble, because he sees the light of this world. 10 But if a man walks in the night, he stumbles, because the light isn't in him." 11 He said these things, and after that, he said to them, "Our friend Lazarus has fallen asleep, but I am going so that I may awake him out of sleep."

12 The disciples therefore said, "Lord, if he has fallen asleep, he will recover."

13 Now Jesus had spoken of his death, but they thought that he spoke of taking rest in sleep. 14 So Jesus said to them plainly then, "Lazarus is dead. 15 I am glad for your sakes that I was not there, so that you may believe. Nevertheless, let's go to him."

16 Thomas therefore, who is called Didymus, said to his fellow disciples, "Let's also go, that we may die with him."

Notes
1. In the Gospel of John, the resurrection of Lazarus is the "sign" or ultimate miracle of Jesus, besides his own resurrection.
2. Sleeping was a common euphemism for dying.

Questions for Reflection, Prayer, and Discussion
1. Do you think Jesus was purposely confusing his disciples?

2. Why did the disciples think they might have to die when they go to Bethany?

READ in your Bible: Jesus Comforts Lazarus' Sisters
John 11:17-37 [WEB]

17 So when Jesus came, he found that he had been in the tomb four days already. 18 Now Bethany was near Jerusalem, about fifteen stadia away. 19 Many of the Jews had joined the women around Martha and Mary, to console them concerning their brother. 20 Then when Martha heard that Jesus was coming, she went and met him, but Mary stayed in the house. 21 Therefore Martha said to Jesus, "Lord, if you would have been here, my brother wouldn't have died. 22 Even now I know that whatever you ask of God, God will give you."

23 Jesus said to her, "Your brother will rise again."

24 Martha said to him, "I know that he will rise again in the resurrection at the last day."

25 Jesus said to her, "I am the resurrection and the life. He who believes in me will still live, even if he dies. 26 Whoever lives and believes in me will never die. Do you believe this?"

27 She said to him, "Yes, Lord. I have come to believe that you are the Christ, God's Son, he who comes into the world."

28 When she had said this, she went away and called Mary, her sister, secretly, saying, "The Teacher is here and is calling you."

29 When she heard this, she arose quickly and went to him. 30 Now Jesus had not yet come into the village, but was in the place where Martha met him. 31 Then the Jews who were with her in the house and were consoling her, when they saw Mary, that she rose up quickly and went out, followed her, saying, "She is going to the tomb to weep there."

32 Therefore when Mary came to where Jesus was and saw him, she fell down at his feet, saying to him, "Lord, if you would have been here, my brother wouldn't have died."

33 When Jesus therefore saw her weeping, and the Jews weeping who came with her, he groaned in the spirit and was troubled, 34 and said, "Where have you laid him?"

They told him, "Lord, come and see."

35 Jesus wept.

36 The Jews therefore said, "See how much affection he had for him!" 37 Some of them said, "Couldn't this man, who opened the eyes of him who was blind, have also kept this man from dying?"

Notes

1. Professional grievers would be hired if an insufficient number of family members were not able to maintain the bereavement period for the full 30 days.
2. "Your brother will rise again" was stated for two purposes. It was a common idiom of support at the moment of a family's bereavement. This was also an affirmation of the common belief about the resurrection on the day of the Last Judgment.
3. Jesus' prayer at the tomb was for the sake of all who were there.

Questions for Reflection, Prayer, and Discussion

1. Do you think that Jesus was as real with Lazarus' sisters as they were with Him? Why do you think so?

2. How does the faith of Mary and Martha make an impression on you?

READ: Jesus Raises Lazarus from Death
John 11:38-44 [WEB]

38 Jesus therefore, again groaning in himself, came to the tomb. Now it was a cave, and a stone lay against it. 39 Jesus said, "Take away the stone."

Martha, the sister of him who was dead, said to him, "Lord, by this time there is a stench, for he has been dead four days."

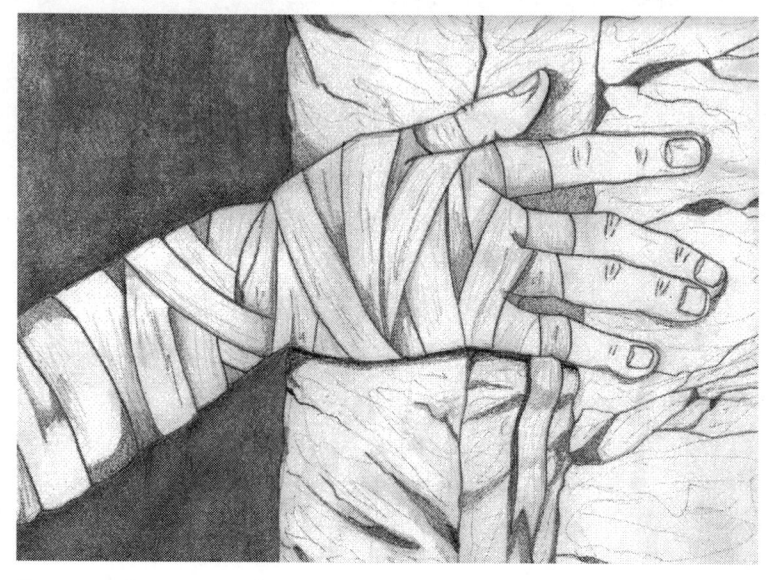

40 Jesus said to her, "Didn't I tell you that if you believed, you would see God's glory?"

41 So they took away the stone from the place where the dead man was lying. Jesus lifted up his eyes and said, "Father, I thank you that you listened to me. 42 I know that you always listen to me, but because of the multitude standing around I said this, that they may believe that you sent me." 43 When he had said this, he cried with a loud voice, "Lazarus, come out!"

44 He who was dead came out, bound hand and foot with wrappings, and his face was wrapped around with a cloth. Jesus said to them, "Free him, and let him go."

Note

It was commonly admitted that when someone died, the spirit lingered close to the body for three days before leaving.

Questions for Reflection, Prayer, and Discussion

1. What are some differences between this resurrection and that of Jesus?

2. What did Jesus do to make sure no one could report this as the action of a magician?

3. What might be a possible reason John shares this, when the other gospels don't mention it?

READ: The Plot to Kill Jesus and Lazarus
John 11:45-57 [WEB]

45 Therefore many of the Jews who came to Mary and saw what Jesus did believed in him. 46 But some of them went away to the Pharisees and told them the things which Jesus had done. 47 The chief priests therefore and the Pharisees gathered a council, and said, "What are we doing? For this man does many signs. 48 If we leave him alone like this, everyone will believe in him, and the Romans will come and take away both our place and our nation."

49 But a certain one of them, Caiaphas, being high priest that year, said to them, "You know nothing at all, 50 nor do you consider that it is advantageous for us that one man should die for the people, and that the whole nation not perish." 51 Now he didn't say this of himself, but being high priest that year, he prophesied that Jesus would die for the nation, 52 and not for the nation only, but that he might also gather together into one the children of God who are scattered abroad. 53 So from that day forward they took counsel that they might put him to death. 54 Jesus therefore walked no more openly among the Jews, but departed from there into the country near the wilderness, to a city called Ephraim. He stayed there with his disciples.

55 Now the Passover of the Jews was at hand. Many went up from the country to Jerusalem before the Passover, to purify themselves. 56 Then they sought for Jesus and spoke with one another as they stood in the temple, "What do you think—that he isn't coming to the feast at all?" 57 Now the chief priests and the Pharisees had commanded that if anyone knew where he was, he should report it, that they might seize him.

Note

The report to the Sanhedrin, the Jewish court of 70 priests, was a turning point in the earthly ministry of Jesus in the eyes of this author of the gospel.

Questions for Reflection, Prayer, and Discussion

1. What were the reasons the Jewish leaders wanted to kill Jesus?

2. What motivated their desire to kill Jesus and Lazarus?

Chapter Twelve
Holiness Brings Forgiveness & Grace

READ: More Than a Dinner
John 12:1-11 [WEB]

1 Then, six days before the Passover, Jesus came to Bethany, where Lazarus was, who had been dead, whom he raised from the dead. 2 So they made him a supper there. Martha served, but Lazarus was one of those who sat at the table with him. 3 Therefore Mary took a pound of ointment of pure nard, very precious, and anointed Jesus's feet and wiped his feet with her hair. The house was filled with the fragrance of the ointment.

4 Then Judas Iscariot, Simon's son, one of his disciples, who would betray him, said, 5 "Why wasn't this ointment sold for three hundred denarii and given to the poor?" 6 Now he said this, not because he cared for the poor, but because he was a thief, and having the money box, used to steal what was put into it.

7 But Jesus said, "Leave her alone. She has kept this for the day of my burial. 8 For you always have the poor with you, but you don't always have me."

9 A large crowd therefore of the Jews learned that he was there; and they came, not for Jesus' sake only, but that they might see Lazarus also, whom he had raised from the dead. 10 But the chief priests conspired to put Lazarus to death also, 11 because on account of him many of the Jews went away and believed in Jesus.

Notes
1. The value of the nard was equal to two years' wages of an ordinary laborer.
2. Nard is an ointment made from the roots and stalks of a plant originating in India. It has a strong spicy perfume, and it is mentioned in the Song of Solomon in the Old Testament.

Questions for Reflection, Prayer, and Discussion
1. Have you ever expressed gratitude to someone by serving him or her in a poignant way?

2. Will using the nard on his feet instead of using the money for the poor affect the lot of the poor in an effective or lasting way?

3. Do you feel that the values of some people today are similar to those of Judas?

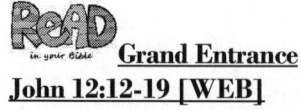

READ in your Bible **Grand Entrance**
John 12:12-19 [WEB]

12 On the next day a great multitude had come to the feast. When they heard that Jesus was coming to Jerusalem, 13 they took the branches of the palm trees and went out to meet him, and cried out, "Hosanna! Blessed is he who comes in the name of the Lord, the King of Israel!"

14 Jesus, having found a young donkey, sat on it. As it is written, 15 "Don't be afraid, daughter of Zion. Behold, your King comes, sitting on a donkey's colt." 16 His disciples didn't understand these things at first, but when Jesus was glorified, then they remembered that these things were written about him, and that they had done these things to him. 17 The multitude therefore that was with him when he called Lazarus out of the tomb and raised him from the dead was testifying about it. 18 For this cause also the multitude went and met him, because they heard that he had done this sign. 19 The Pharisees therefore said among themselves, "See how you accomplish nothing. Behold, the world has gone after him."

Notes

1. The word **Hosanna** is the Latin transliteration of a Hebrew word that is a call to divine help and a shout of jubilation.
2. The expression, "in the Lord's name," means "with God's full authority."
3. The entry of Jesus on a colt was an act of humility, which may have provided some of the reason why the Jews did not accept him as Messiah. Traditionally, a great leader would enter a horse.

Questions for Reflection, Prayer, and Discussion

1. Jesus' arrival in Jerusalem was important to the crowd. How is it important to His followers today?

2. How do you think the temple's leaders reacted to His grand entrance?

3. How does Jesus' entrance into Jerusalem reflect His unique holiness?

Seekers and Messengers
John 12:20-26 [WEB]

20 Now there were certain Greeks among those who went up to worship at the feast. 21 Therefore, these came to Philip, who was from Bethsaida of Galilee, and asked him, saying, "Sir, we want to see Jesus." 22 Philip came and told Andrew, and in turn, Andrew came with Philip, and they told Jesus.

23 Jesus answered them, "The time has come for the Son of Man to be glorified. 24 Most certainly I tell you, unless a grain of wheat falls into the earth and dies, it remains by itself alone. But if it dies, it bears much fruit. 25 He who loves his life will lose it. He who hates his life in this world will keep it to eternal life. 26 If anyone serves me, let him follow me. Where I am, there my servant will also be. If anyone serves me, the Father will honor him.

Note
Identifying the seekers as Greeks was a euphemism for Gentiles.

A Question for Reflection, Prayer, and Discussion
Were Philip and Andrew simply messengers, or do you think they did more here that is not mentioned?

Some Said It Thundered
John 12:27-36a [WEB]

27 "Now my soul is troubled. What shall I say? 'Father, save me from this time?' But I came to this time for this cause. 28 Father, glorify your name!"

Then a voice came out of the sky, saying, "I have both glorified it and will glorify it again."

29 Therefore the multitude who stood by and heard it said that it had thundered. Others said, "An angel has spoken to him."

30 Jesus answered, "This voice hasn't come for my sake, but for your sakes. 31 Now is the judgment of this world. Now the prince of this world will be cast out. 32 And I, if I am lifted up from the earth, will draw all people to myself." 33 But he said this, signifying by what kind of death he should die.

34 The multitude answered him, "We have heard out of the law that the Christ remains forever. How do you say, 'The Son of Man must be lifted up?' Who is this Son of Man?"

35 Jesus therefore said to them, "Yet a little while the light is with you. Walk while you have the light, that darkness doesn't overtake you. He who walks in the darkness doesn't know where he is going. 36 While you have the light, believe in the light, that you may become children of light."

Notes

1. It is clear that only Jesus and his inner circle of disciples heard the voice in the midst of the thunder.
2. For John, the time of "signs" or miracles is basically over, so now either people respond to His coming, or they don't.

Questions for Reflection, Prayer, and Discussion

1. Do you sense intimacy in this conversation between the Savior of our faith and God our Father?

2. What are some differences you see between the ways Jesus and Satan relate to the world?

READ Prophecy Fulfilled
John 12:36b-43 [WEB]

Jesus said these things, and he departed and hid himself from them. 37 But though he had done so many signs before them, yet they didn't believe in him, 38 that the word of Isaiah the prophet might be fulfilled, which he spoke: "Lord, who has believed our report? To whom has the arm of the Lord been revealed?"

39 For this cause they couldn't believe, for Isaiah said again: 40 "He has blinded their eyes and he hardened their heart, lest they should see with their eyes, and perceive with their heart, and would turn, and I would heal them."

41 Isaiah said these things when he saw his glory, and spoke of him. 42 Nevertheless, even many of the rulers believed in him, but because of the Pharisees they didn't confess it, so that they wouldn't be put out of the synagogue, 43 for they loved men's praise more than God's praise.

Notes
1. In John, the refusal to believe in the signs and holiness of Jesus was spiritual harshness or blindness, although proscription against the teachings of Jesus condemned those who outlawed them.
2. Of the authorities who believed in Him, the only ones listed in the Bible were Joseph of Aramethea and Nicodemus.

Questions for Reflection, Prayer, and Discussion
1. Are there people you know who do not embrace Jesus as their Savior? What are their reasons?

2. As a response, what are some reasons for embracing Jesus as your Savior?

ReAD in your Bible An Affirmation of Faith
John 12:44-50

44 Jesus cried out and said, "Whoever believes in me, believes not in me, but in him who sent me. 45 He who sees me sees him who sent me. 46 I have come as a light into the world, that whoever believes in me may not remain in the darkness. 47 If anyone listens to my sayings and doesn't believe, I don't judge him. For I came not to judge the world, but to save the world. 48 He who rejects me, and doesn't receive my sayings, has one who judges him. The word that I spoke will judge him in the last day. 49 For I spoke not from myself, but the Father who sent me gave me a commandment, what I should say and what I should speak. 50 I know that his commandment is eternal life. The things therefore which I speak, even as the Father has said to me, so I speak."

Questions for Reflection, Prayer, and Discussion
1. Is this a summary of what we already know, or does Jesus seem to be saying something different here?

2. What emotions, if any, do you sense in Jesus as he makes these statements?

3. Why do you think John includes this, while the other gospels do not?

Chapter Thirteen
Holiness Has Focus

An Act of Servitude
John 13:1-11 [WEB]

1 Now before the feast of the Passover, Jesus, knowing that his time had come that he would depart from this world to the Father, having loved his own who were in the world, he loved them to the end. 2 During supper, the devil having already put into the heart of Judas Iscariot, Simon's son, to betray him, 3 Jesus, knowing that the Father had given all things into his hands, and that he came from God and was going to God, 4 arose from supper, and laid aside his outer garments. He took a towel and wrapped a towel around his waist. 5 Then he poured water into the basin, and began to wash the disciples' feet and to wipe them with the towel that was wrapped around him. 6 Then he came to Simon Peter. He said to him, "Lord, do you wash my feet?"

7 Jesus answered him, "You don't know what I am doing now, but you will understand later."

8 Peter said to him, "You will never wash my feet!"

Jesus answered him, "If I don't wash you, you have no part with me."

9 Simon Peter said to him, "Lord, not my feet only, but also my hands and my head!"

10 Jesus said to him, "Someone who has bathed only needs to have his feet washed, but is completely clean. You are clean, but not all of you." 11 For he knew him who would betray him; therefore he said, "You are not all clean."

Notes

1. Unwritten rules of hospitality demanded that the host of a meal provide services at the door that would make the guests comfortable. These services may include the foot bath, the anointing of the head with oil, and the provision of a hug among other opportunities.
2. Just as the other evangelists, John clearly shows how much Jesus knew those who were close to Him. Note that Judas is loved and is part of the inner circle, though Jesus knew what Judas would do.

Questions for Reflection, Prayer, and Discussion

1. Have you ever felt humbled by someone else's serving your needs?

2. Do you prefer to serve or to be served? Why?

3. Is Jesus demonstrating a holiness that He wants His followers to pursue? Why do you think so?

ReAD: Teaching from Example
John 13:12-20 [WEB]

12 So when he had washed their feet, put his outer garment back on, and sat down again, he said to them, "Do you know what I have done to you? 13 You call me, 'Teacher' and 'Lord.' You say so correctly, for so I am. 14 If I then, the Lord and the Teacher, have washed your feet, you also ought to wash one another's feet. 15 For I have given you an example, that you should also do as I have done to you. 16 Most certainly I tell you, a servant is not greater than his lord, neither is one who is sent greater than he who sent him. 17 If you know these things, blessed are you if you do them. 18 I don't speak concerning all of you. I know whom I have chosen; but that the Scripture may be fulfilled, 'He who eats bread with me has lifted up his heel against me.' 19 From now on, I tell you before it happens, that when it happens, you may believe that I am he. 20 Most certainly I tell you, he who receives whomever I send, receives me; and he who receives me, receives him who sent me."

Notes

1. Jesus seems to indicate plainly that he indicates a sense of direction and an attitude. It is not imperative to wash each other's feet every time they break bread together.
2. The relationship between the servant and the master, and between giving and receiving, is used by Jesus to show how his disciples should deal with one another.

Questions for Reflection, Prayer, and Discussion

1. If you place yourself in the sandals of those listening to Him, what differences do you see between the way you relate to Jesus, and the way you relate to the others in the upper room?

2. When you look at Judas seated nearby, do you think Jesus loves him? Could you love him as Jesus does?

3. What are some of the reasons that Christians may stumble and cease to be faithful followers of Jesus?

READ **The Act of Betrayal**
John 13:21-30 [WEB]

21 When Jesus had said this, he was troubled in spirit, and testified, "Most certainly I tell you that one of you will betray me."

22 The disciples looked at one another, perplexed about whom he spoke. 23 One of his disciples, whom Jesus loved, was at the table, leaning against Jesus' breast. 24 Simon Peter therefore beckoned to him, and said to him, "Tell us who it is of whom he speaks."

25 He, leaning back, as he was, on Jesus' breast, asked him, "Lord, who is it?"

26 Jesus therefore answered, "It is he to whom I will give this piece of bread when I have dipped it." So when he had dipped the piece of bread, he gave it to Judas, the son of Simon Iscariot. 27 After the piece of bread, then Satan entered into him.

Then Jesus said to him, "What you do, do quickly."

28 Now nobody at the table knew why he said this to him. 29 For some thought, because Judas had the money box, that Jesus said to him, "Buy what things we need for the feast," or that he should give something to the poor. 30 Therefore having received that morsel, he went out immediately. It was night.

Notes

1. Jesus is fully aware of the evil at work in Judas, but the remainder of his inner circle is oblivious to what is happening.
2. Throughout the New Testament, Satan continues to have a distinct personality.

Questions for Reflection, Prayer, and Discussion

1. Why do you suppose Jesus makes the offering to Judas?

2. Why might Judas be so vulnerable to Satan's influence?

3. Is John's portrayal of Judas helpful in your understanding Jesus' relationship to Judas? Why?

Jesus Calls for Love
John 13:31-35 [WEB]

31 When he had gone out, Jesus said, "Now the Son of Man has been glorified, and God has been glorified in him. 32 If God has been glorified in him, God will also glorify him in himself, and he will glorify him immediately. 33 Little children, I will be with you a little while longer. You will seek me, and as I said to the Jews, 'Where I am going, you can't come,' so now I tell you. 34 A new commandment I give to you, that you love one another. Just as I have loved you, you also love one another. 35 By this everyone will know that you are my disciples, if you have love for one another."

Questions for Reflection, Prayer, and Discussion

1. Why do you suppose Jesus calls for love immediately after Judas leaves?

2. Why will the bonds of love be so important in the aftermath of Jesus' Passion?

READ Peter Makes a Request
John 13:36-38 [WEB]
36 Simon Peter said to him, "Lord, where are you going?"

Jesus answered, "Where I am going, you can't follow now, but you will follow afterwards."

37 Peter said to him, "Lord, why can't I follow you now? I will lay down my life for you."

38 Jesus answered him, "Will you lay down your life for me? Most certainly I tell you, the rooster won't crow until you have denied me three times.

Questions for Reflection, Prayer, and Discussion
1. Is Peter's question out of place in this setting? Why?

2. Is Peter's question one of curiosity, or is it a gesture of leadership? Why do you think so?

3. Could Peter's question show a measure of insecurity on his part?

4. Does Jesus' answer reflect doubt of Peter's loyalty? Why?

Chapter Fourteen
Holiness Loves

READ: Jesus Comforts His Disciples
John 14:1-4 [WEB]

"Don't let your heart be troubled. Believe in God. Believe also in me. 2 In my Father's house are many homes. If it weren't so, I would have told you. I am going to prepare a place for you. 3 If I go and prepare a place for you, I will come again and will receive you to myself; that where I am, you may be there also. 4 You know where I go, and you know the way."

Notes

1. Clearly, Jesus reassures his followers when they start to realize that disaster may be imminent.
2. Question [2b] can also be translated as a statement. ". . [...] I would tell you, because I am going to prepare a place. . .."
3. The clear commandment [1b] can be translated as well, "You believe in God..." Belief in God has now become much more personal in Jesus.

Questions for Reflection, Prayer, and Discussion

1. Does this description of fellowship with God in the larger life relate to how you fellowship with Jesus now?

2. How does Jesus' preparing a place for you and coming for you affect your attitude towards Him?

3. Do you see Him more as suffering servant or as Master?

Questions and Requests from the Apostles
John 14:5-14 [WEB]

5 Thomas said to him, "Lord, we don't know where you are going. How can we know the way?"

6 Jesus said to him, "I am the way, the truth, and the life. No one comes to the Father, except through me. 7 If you had known me, you would have known my Father also. From now on, you know him and have seen him."

8 Philip said to him, "Lord, show us the Father, and that will be enough for us."

9 Jesus said to him, "Have I been with you such a long time, and do you not know me, Philip? He who has seen me has seen the Father. How do you say, 'Show us the Father?' 10 Don't you believe that I am in the Father, and the Father in me? The words that I tell you, I speak not from myself; but the Father who lives in me does his works. 11 Believe me that I am in the Father, and the Father in me; or else believe me for the very works' sake. 12 Most certainly I tell you, he who believes in me, the works that I do, he will do also; and he will do greater works than these, because I am going to my Father. 13 Whatever you will ask in my name, I will do it, that the Father may be glorified in the Son. 14 If you will ask anything in my name, I will do it.

Notes

1. Jesus' reply to Thomas bears witness to an exclusive access to God through Jesus. The knowledge of God therefore passes by the personality, actions and teachings of Jesus.
2. Prayer is the channel through which much more will be fulfilled after Jesus has been glorified and the Holy Spirit has been given to Jesus' followers at Pentecost.
3. To ask in His name means to ask with His authority and with His will at the same time.

Questions for Reflection, Prayer, and Discussion

1. Does knowing Jesus better through John's testimony help you feel closer to God?

2. What approach do you take to prayer to get the results you hope for?

Holy Spirit Promised
John 14:15-17 [WEB]

15 If you love me, keep my commandments. 16 I will pray to the Father, and he will give you another Counselor, that he may be with you forever: 17 the Spirit of truth, whom the world can't receive, for it doesn't see him and doesn't know him. You know him, for he lives with you and will be in you.

Notes

1. The term *advocate* [NRSV and NIV] is sometimes translated *helper* [NASB, NKJV and ESV] or *counselor*. The Greek term is *paraclete*, which can be strongly associated with the British legal system's advocate, who does not simply defend the client, but speaks for and stands on behalf of the client in a more literal and intimate way than does an American lawyer.
2. The Greek word *meno*, is translated "abide" in older translations, which is an outdated word that has no direct equivalent in contemporary English. The Greek term meno, has a much richer meaning than simply "remain" or "live", which are the words used for meno in new translations. John further uses the term meno in the following chapter.

Questions for Reflection, Prayer, and Discussion

1. Do you experience the Holy Spirit as truth, or do you have another way to describe it?

2. Can you describe how the Holy Spirit that Jesus provides works within you?

ReAD Promise of Fellowship
John 14:18-24 [WEB]

18 I will not leave you orphans. I will come to you. 19 Yet a little while, and the world will see me no more; but you will see me. Because I live, you will live also. 20 In that day you will know that I am in my Father, and you in me, and I in you. 21 One who has my commandments and keeps them, that person is one who loves me. One who loves me will be loved by my Father, and I will love him, and will reveal myself to him."

22 Judas (not Iscariot) said to him, "Lord, what has happened that you are about to reveal yourself to us, and not to the world?"

23 Jesus answered him, "If a man loves me, he will keep my word. My Father will love him, and we will come to him and make our home with him. 24 He who doesn't love me doesn't keep my words. The word which you hear isn't mine, but the Father's who sent me.

Notes
1. The life of Christ is an integral part of the Holy Spirit that helps us to connect with God.
2. Slavery to Christ is bound by love for him.

Questions for Reflection, Prayer, and Discussion
1. Does fellowship begin with accepting Him as Savior, or after one goes on to the larger life? Why do you think so?

2. If love for Christ separates His followers from the rest of the world at earthly death, what are some ways to introduce people to the love of Christ?

ReAD More on the Advocate
John 14:25-31 [WEB]

25 "I have said these things to you while still living with you. 26 But the Counselor, the Holy Spirit, whom the Father will send in my name, will teach you all things, and will remind you of all that I said to you. 27 Peace I leave with you. My peace I give to you; not as the world gives, I give to you. Don't let your heart be troubled, neither let it be fearful. 28 You heard how I told you, 'I am going away, and I will come back to you.' If you loved me, you would have rejoiced because I said 'I am going to my Father;' for the Father is greater than I. 29 Now I have told you before it happens so that when it happens, you may believe. 30 I will no more speak much with you, for the prince of the world comes, and he has nothing in

me. 31 But that the world may know that I love the Father, and as the Father commanded me, even so I do. Arise, let's go from here.

Notes
1. When the Holy Spirit helps us to comprehend His teachings, one consequence is peace.
2. The conflict with Satan culminates in the fact that Satan's power is destroyed by the Resurrection.

Questions for Reflection, Prayer, and Discussion
1. When you pray about a situation, do you always pray until you have peace before you draw conclusions, or do you have any other stopping point?

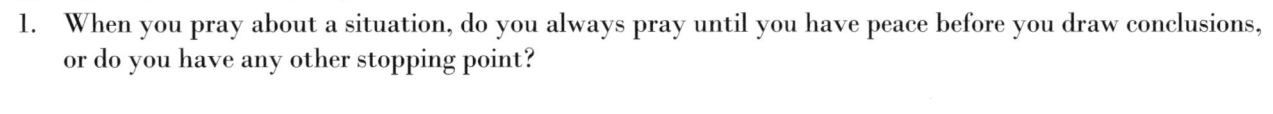

2. How does prayer affect your situation as you seek fellowship with Christ?

3. Do you always find peace when you seek God's presence?

Questions for Further Reflection and Discussion

The twelve apostles have been living and working with Jesus about three years now. In what ways do you now see them reflecting some of Jesus' holiness?

Jesus knows that He soon will be going home to our Father in Heaven. Consider the ways they are ready to go on without Him and the ways they need further preparation. Discuss those things here.

In God's school of holiness our Lord Jesus Christ (the Father's Son and the Christian's Savior) is with us, and we with Him, in a controlling relationship of master and servant, leader and follower, teacher and student.

Packer, J. I.. *Rediscovering Holiness*
(p. 16). Baker Publishing Group.
Kindle Edition.

Chapter Fifteen
Holiness Provides

READ **The Command to Abide/Remain**

John 15:1-11 [WEB]

1 "I am the true vine, and my Father is the farmer. 2 Every branch in me that doesn't bear fruit, he takes away. Every branch that bears fruit, he prunes, that it may bear more fruit. 3 You are already pruned clean because of the word which I have spoken to you. 4 Remain in me, and I in you. As the branch can't bear fruit by itself unless it remains in the vine, so neither can you, unless you remain in me. 5 I am the vine. You are the branches. He who remains in me and I in him bears much fruit, for apart from me you can do nothing. 6 If a man doesn't remain in me, he is thrown out as a branch and is withered; and they gather them, throw them into the fire, and they are burned. 7 If you remain in me, and my words remain in you, you will ask whatever you desire, and it will be done for you.

8 "In this my Father is glorified, that you bear much fruit; and so you will be my disciples. 9 Even as the Father has loved me, I also have loved you. Remain in my love. 10 If you keep my commandments, you will remain in my love, even as I have kept my Father's commandments and remain in his love. 11 I have spoken these things to you, that my joy may remain in you, and that your joy may be made full.

Notes

1. Jesus being the true vine [1] is a reference to those days when Jeremiah called the people of God a wild vine. Jeremiah 2:21 [NRSV] says, "Yet I planted you as a choice vine, from the purest stock. How then did you turn degenerate and become a wild vine?"
2. The vine grower is, more literally, vine dresser. [1] When the vine grower prunes the vines, a literal translation would say he cleans the vines, removing all the fallen leaves and branches. This gives further meaning to Jesus' saying, "You are already made clean...."
3. Grapevine wood, even in a larger diameter, is completely useless except as fuel for a fire. For this, it is barely good enough to bring heat, since it does not produce the desired embers for cooking. [6]

Questions for Reflection, Prayer, and Discussion

1. What does one do to have the sense of abiding or living in Jesus and not merely praying?

2. What difference do you see between abiding in Jesus and simply accepting Him as your savior?

3. If you are abiding in the vine of Jesus, in what ways are you growing?

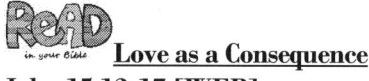

Love as a Consequence
John 15:12-17 [WEB]

12 "This is my commandment, that you love one another, even as I have loved you. 13 Greater love has no one than this, that someone lay down his life for his friends. 14 You are my friends if you do whatever I command you. 15 No longer do I call you servants, for the servant doesn't know what his lord does. But I have called you friends, for everything that I heard from my Father, I have made known to you. 16 You didn't choose me, but I chose you and appointed you, that you should go and bear fruit, and that your fruit should remain; that whatever you will ask of the Father in my name, he may give it to you. 17 "I command these things to you, that you may love one another.

Notes
1. By "abiding in him," they will love one another as He has loved them.
2. By "abiding in him," we are no longer in contact with him as servants, but as friends – friends of Jesus.

Questions for Reflection, Prayer, and Discussion
1. What differences do you see between simply loving one another and loving in connection with the abiding love of Christ?

2. Is there a difference between the fruit simply born of a human relationship and the fruit born of a mutual relationship with Christ?

3. Since God is love [1 John 4:8, 16], does having Jesus in your heart help move you towards holiness?

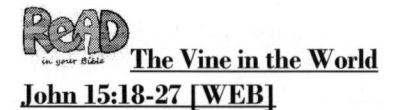

Read The Vine in the World
John 15:18-27 [WEB]

18 If the world hates you, you know that it has hated me before it hated you. 19 If you were of the world, the world would love its own. But because you are not of the world, since I chose you out of the world, therefore the world hates you. 20 Remember the word that I said to you: 'A servant is not greater than his lord.' If they persecuted me, they will also persecute you. If they kept my word, they will also keep yours. 21 But they will do all these things to you for my name's sake, because they don't know him who sent me. 22 If I had not come and spoken to them, they would not have had sin; but now they have no excuse for their sin. 23 He who hates me, hates my Father also. 24 If I hadn't done among them the works which no one else did, they wouldn't have had sin. But now they have seen and also hated both me and my Father. 25 But this happened so that the word may be fulfilled which was written in their law, 'They hated me without a cause.'

26 "When the Counselor has come, whom I will send to you from the Father, the Spirit of truth, who proceeds from the Father, he will testify about me. 27 You will also testify, because you have been with me from the beginning.

Notes

1. In the face of Jesus' difficult teachings, the world rejects Him. Consequently, when we confront the world with these same teachings, we sometimes get the same hostile reception.
2. Throughout the Bible, the word translated servant is more precisely translated slave. At the time, the enslavement of Israel looked more like a contract servant, in that legally all slaves were to be released every seventh year into normal family security in most cases.

Questions for Reflection, Prayer, and Discussion

1. Do you know anyone who simply cannot accept the teachings of Jesus?

2. Did you ever experience any real hostility towards Christians and Christianity? If so, describe it.

3. Does abiding or remaining in the True Vine help you stand against the evils of our world? How?

Chapter Sixteen
Holiness Is Timeless

Conflict to Come
John 16:1-4a [WEB]

1 "I have said these things to you so that you wouldn't be caused to stumble. 2 They will put you out of the synagogues. Yes, the time is coming that whoever kills you will think that he offers service to God. 3 They will do these things because they have not known the Father nor me. 4 But I have told you these things so that when the time comes, you may remember that I told you about them.

Questions for Reflection, Prayer, and Discussion

1. Have you witnessed actual conflict between Christians and non-Christians, either in person or on television? If so, describe what you saw and your reactions?

2. Can you give examples where sometimes Christians cause conflict with actions that Jesus would prohibit?

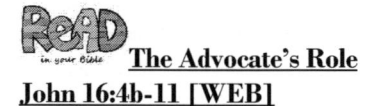

The Advocate's Role
John 16:4b-11 [WEB]

I didn't tell you these things from the beginning, because I was with you. 5 But now I am going to him who sent me, and none of you asks me, 'Where are you going?' 6 But because I have told you these things, sorrow has filled your heart. 7 Nevertheless I tell you the truth: It is to your advantage that I go away; for if I don't go away, the Counselor won't come to you. But if I go, I will send him to you. 8 When he has come, he will convict the world about sin, about righteousness, and about judgment; 9 about sin, because they don't believe in me; 10 about righteousness, because I am going to my Father, and you won't see me any more; 11 about judgment, because the prince of this world has been judged.

Notes

1. Jesus plainly declares that the true work of the **Advocate** in their lives will begin after His death. In a sense, the resurrection releases the power of the Holy Spirit into the lives of his disciples, which was manifested at Pentecost in the Book of Acts.

2. Jesus brings their imminent mourning into perspective to help them face what is about to happen.

Questions for Reflection, Prayer, and Discussion

1. Can you describe ways the Holy Spirit proves the world wrong in your life?

2. How do you see yourself set apart in terms of sin, righteousness, and judgment?

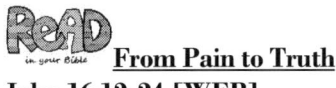

READ From Pain to Truth
John 16:12-24 [WEB]

12 "I still have many things to tell you, but you can't bear them now. 13 However, when he, the Spirit of truth, has come, he will guide you into all truth, for he will not speak from himself; but whatever he hears, he will speak. He will declare to you things that are coming. 14 He will glorify me, for he will take from what is mine and will declare it to you. 15 All things that the Father has are mine; therefore I said that he takes of mine and will declare it to you.

16 "A little while, and you will not see me. Again a little while, and you will see me."

17 Some of his disciples therefore said to one another, "What is this that he says to us, 'A little while, and you won't see me, and again a little while, and you will see me;' and, 'Because I go to the Father'?" 18 They said therefore, "What is this that he says, 'A little while'? We don't know what he is saying."

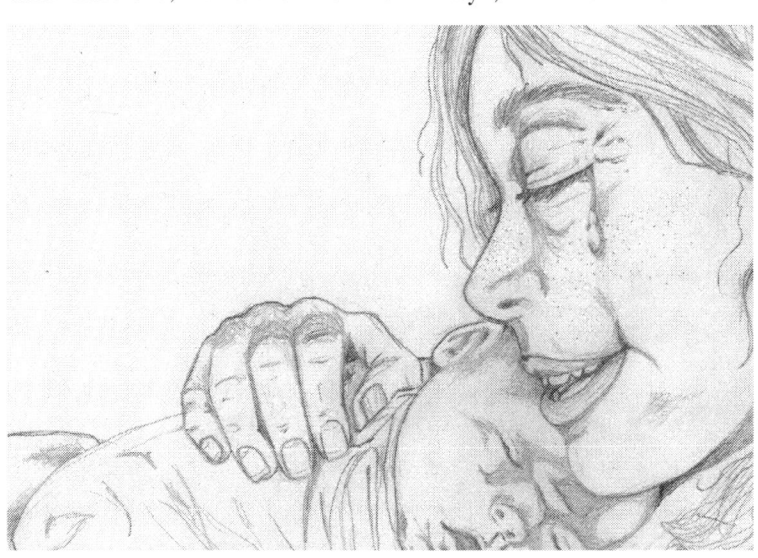

19 Therefore Jesus perceived that they wanted to ask him, and he said to them, "Do you inquire among yourselves concerning this, that I said, 'A little while, and you won't see me, and again a little while, and you will see me?' 20 Most certainly I tell you that you will weep and lament, but the world will rejoice. You will be sorrowful, but your sorrow will be turned into joy. 21 A woman, when she gives birth, has sorrow because her time has come. But when she has delivered the child, she doesn't remember the anguish any more, for the joy that a human being is born into the world. 22 Therefore you now have sorrow, but I will see you again, and your heart will rejoice, and no one will take your joy away from you.

23 "In that day you will ask me no questions. Most certainly I tell you, whatever you may ask of the Father in my name, he will give it to you. 24 Until now, you have asked nothing in my name. Ask, and you will receive, that your joy may be made full.

Notes
1. The Spirit/Advocate is the key to the believer's understanding of what God does in Christ.
2. The birth metaphor is provided as a tool to understand what is about to happen.

Questions for Reflection, Prayer, and Discussion
1. Can you describe times you have had a sense of the Holy Spirit helping you to understand something?

2. When you are in pain, how do you approach God in prayer?

3. Do you think the Holy Spirit is helping you as you work through this study of John's gospel, helping you approach holiness?

READ in your Bible: The Promise of Triumph
John 16:25-33 [WEB]

25 "I have spoken these things to you in figures of speech. But the time is coming when I will no more speak to you in figures of speech, but will tell you plainly about the Father. 26 In that day you will ask in my name; and I don't say to you that I will pray to the Father for you, 27 for the Father himself loves you, because you have loved me, and have believed that I came from God. 28 I came from the Father and have come into the world. Again, I leave the world and go to the Father."

29 His disciples said to him, "Behold, now you are speaking plainly, and using no figures of speech. 30 Now we know that you know all things, and don't need for anyone to question you. By this we believe that you came from God."

31 Jesus answered them, "Do you now believe? 32 Behold, the time is coming, yes, and has now come, that you will be scattered, everyone to his own place, and you will leave me alone. Yet I am not alone,

because the Father is with me. 33 I have told you these things, that in me you may have peace. In the world you have trouble; but cheer up! I have overcome the world."

Questions for Reflection, Prayer, and Discussion

1. Since He has just made clear His imminent death, in what ways was what He said useful for them?

2. Has Jesus already conquered the world at this point? If you think so, what is your witness as to why?

3. Are you tempted to tell people that, by following Jesus and trying to be like Him, that you are approaching His holiness? Why?

Chapter Seventeen
Holiness Through Prayer

Jesus Prays for the Fulfillment of His Mission in Glory
John 17:1-5 [WEB]

1 Jesus said these things, then lifting up his eyes to heaven, he said, "Father, the time has come. Glorify your Son, that your Son may also glorify you; 2 even as you gave him authority over all flesh, so he will give eternal life to all whom you have given him. 3 This is eternal life, that they should know you, the only true God, and him whom you sent, Jesus Christ. 4 I glorified you on the earth. I have accomplished the work which you have given me to do. 5 Now, Father, glorify me with your own self with the glory which I had with you before the world existed.

Notes

1. This is the first segment of Jesus' most wide-ranging prayer in John's gospel.
2. This chapter is a "high priestly" prayer in the sense that it intercedes on behalf of all those in His direct care.

Question for Reflection, Prayer, and Discussion

What does this opening to His prayer tell you about Jesus' mood, His emotions, and His sense of mission?

Jesus Prays for His Disciples
John 17:6-19 [WEB]

6 "I revealed your name to the people whom you have given me out of the world. They were yours, and you have given them to me. They have kept your word. 7 Now they have known that all things whatever you have given me are from you, 8 for the words which you have given me I have given to them; and they received them, and knew for sure that I came from you. They have believed that you sent me. 9 I pray for them. I don't pray for the world, but for those whom you have given me, for they are yours. 10 All things that are mine are yours, and yours are mine, and I am glorified in them. 11 I am no more in the world, but these are in the world, and I am coming to you. Holy Father, keep them through your name which you have given me, that they may be one, even as we are. 12 While I was with them in the world, I kept them in your name. I have kept those whom you have given me. None of them is lost except the son of destruction, that the Scripture might be fulfilled. 13 But now I come to you, and I say these things in the world, that they may have my joy made full in themselves. 14 I have given them your word. The world hated them because they are not of the world, even as I am not of the world. 15 I pray not that you would take them from the world, but that you would keep them from the evil one. 16 They are not of the world, even as I am not of the world. 17 Sanctify them in your truth. Your word is truth. 18 As you sent

me into the world, even so I have sent them into the world. 19 For their sakes I sanctify myself, that they themselves also may be sanctified in truth.

Questions for Reflection, Prayer, and Discussion

1. When Jesus prays for His disciples, what is the prayer's focus, and how are we part of His focus?

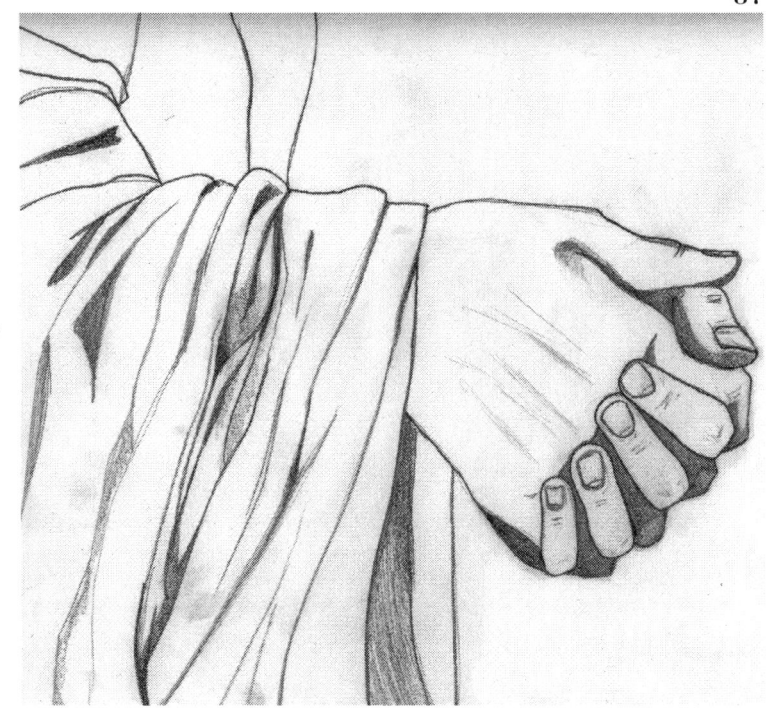

2. How frequently do you pray for your church or faith community?

ReAD **Jesus Prays for All Who Believe He is Their Savior**
John 17:20-26 [WEB]

20 "Not for these only do I pray, but for those also who will believe in me through their word, 21 that they may all be one; even as you, Father, are in me, and I in you, that they also may be one in us; that the world may believe that you sent me. 22 The glory which you have given me, I have given to them, that they may be one, even as we are one, 23 I in them, and you in me, that they may be perfected into one, that the world may know that you sent me and loved them, even as you loved me. 24 Father, I desire that they also whom you have given me be with me where I am, that they may see my glory which you have given me, for you loved me before the foundation of the world. 25 Righteous Father, the world hasn't known you, but I knew you; and these knew that you sent me. 26 I made known to them your name, and will make it known; that the love with which you loved me may be in them, and I in them."

Questions for Reflection, Prayer, and Discussion

1. When Jesus prays for the whole worldwide church, how is this a good example for us to follow?

2. How do you approach praying for all Christians, even beyond your own local spiritual community?

3. As you pray for the larger church, are you willing to try to reflect Jesus' holiness as you pray?

Chapter Eighteen
Holiness Is Dependable

Valley Confrontation
John 18:1-11 [WEB]

When Jesus had spoken these words, he went out with his disciples over the brook Kidron, where there was a garden, into which he and his disciples entered. 2 Now Judas, who betrayed him, also knew the place, for Jesus often met there with his disciples. 3 Judas then, having taken a detachment of soldiers and officers from the chief priests and the Pharisees, came there with lanterns, torches, and weapons. 4 Jesus therefore, knowing all the things that were happening to him, went out and said to them, "Who are you looking for?"

5 They answered him, "Jesus of Nazareth."

Jesus said to them, "I am he."

Judas also, who betrayed him, was standing with them. 6 When therefore he said to them, "I am he," they went backward and fell to the ground.

7 Again therefore he asked them, "Who are you looking for?"

They said, "Jesus of Nazareth."

8 Jesus answered, "I told you that I am he. If therefore you seek me, let these go their way," 9 that the word might be fulfilled which he spoke, "Of those whom you have given me, I have lost none."

10 Simon Peter therefore, having a sword, drew it, struck the high priest's servant, and cut off his right ear. The servant's name was Malchus. 11 Jesus therefore said to Peter, "Put the sword into its sheath. The cup which the Father has given me, shall I not surely drink it?"

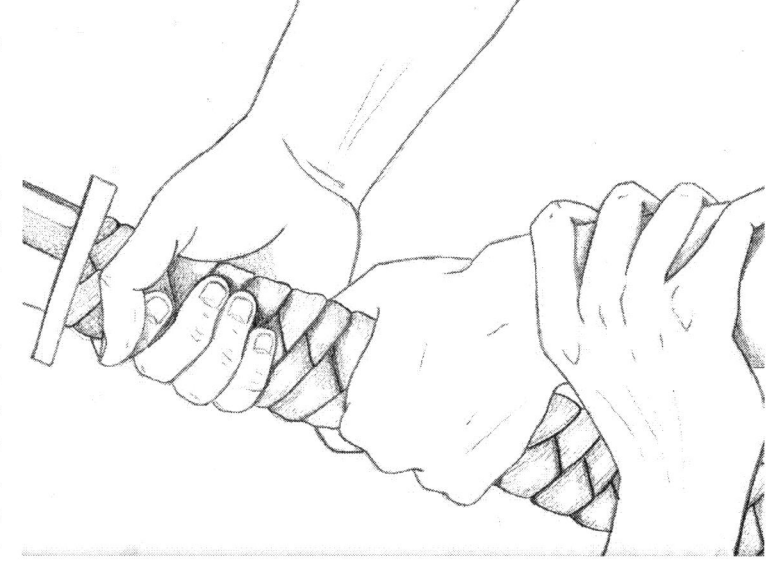

Notes

1. In the deep darkness of the night, the Temple authorities needed Judas to guide the soldiers towards Jesus and identify him.
2. Judas is mentioned here for the last time on the Gospel of John.

Questions for Reflection, Prayer, and Discussion

1. Why might John exclude the struggle, dialogue, and prayers in the Garden found in the other three gospels?

2. What aspects of Jesus' holiness do you observe here?

3. How do you think the other eleven disciples are reacting to Judas, who had been part of their lives for three years?

READ in your Bible — Arrest and Appearance Before Annas
John 18:12-23 [WEB]

12 So the detachment, the commanding officer, and the officers of the Jews seized Jesus and bound him, 13 and led him to Annas first, for he was father-in-law to Caiaphas, who was high priest that year. 14 Now it was Caiaphas who advised the Jews that it was expedient that one man should perish for the people.

15 Simon Peter followed Jesus, as did another disciple. Now that disciple was known to the high priest, and entered in with Jesus into the court of the high priest; 16 but Peter was standing at the door outside. So the other disciple, who was known to the high priest, went out and spoke to her who kept the door, and brought in Peter. 17 Then the maid who kept the door said to Peter, "Are you also one of this man's disciples?"

He said, "I am not."

18 Now the servants and the officers were standing there, having made a fire of coals, for it was cold. They were warming themselves. Peter was with them, standing and warming himself.

19 The high priest therefore asked Jesus about his disciples and about his teaching.

20 Jesus answered him, "I spoke openly to the world. I always taught in synagogues and in the temple, where the Jews always meet. I said nothing in secret. 21 Why do you ask me? Ask those who have heard me what I said to them. Behold, they know the things which I said."

22 When he had said this, one of the officers standing by slapped Jesus with his hand, saying, "Do you answer the high priest like that?"

23 Jesus answered him, "If I have spoken evil, testify of the evil; but if well, why do you beat me?"

Questions for Reflection, Prayer, and Discussion

1. Why might John want his readers to know about this appearance before Annas along with Peter's first denial, since it is an encounter not mentioned in the other gospels?

2. What do you learn about the politics of Jesus' arrest from this event?

Jesus Before Caiaphas and Two More Denials
John 18:24-27 [WEB]

24 Annas sent him bound to Caiaphas, the high priest.

25 Now Simon Peter was standing and warming himself. They said therefore to him, "You aren't also one of his disciples, are you?"

He denied it and said, "I am not."

26 One of the servants of the high priest, being a relative of him whose ear Peter had cut off, said, "Didn't I see you in the garden with him?"

27 Peter therefore denied it again, and immediately the rooster crowed.

Questions for Reflection, Prayer, and Discussion

1. Does Peter let His Lord down with these three denials? Why do you think so?

2. Have you ever avoided admitting you are a follower of Jesus Christ?

Jesus Taken Before Pilate
John 18:28-32 [WEB]

28 They led Jesus therefore from Caiaphas into the Praetorium. It was early, and they themselves didn't enter into the Praetorium, that they might not be defiled, but might eat the Passover. 29 Pilate therefore went out to them and said, "What accusation do you bring against this man?"

30 They answered him, "If this man weren't an evildoer, we wouldn't have delivered him up to you."

31 Pilate therefore said to them, "Take him yourselves, and judge him according to your law."

Therefore the Jews said to him, "It is illegal for us to put anyone to death," 32 that the word of Jesus might be fulfilled, which he spoke, signifying by what kind of death he should die.

Notes

1. Entering the headquarters of Pilate, the house of a Gentile, would render the religious leaders formally unclean.
2. Local authorities in the Roman Empire were not able to apply the death penalty. The Jewish execution would have meant stoning. Crucifixion was the Empire's favorite method for criminals.

Questions for Reflection, Prayer, and Discussion

1. What kind of emotions evidently pushed the religious leaders to take such drastic action?

2. How do you suppose they felt, using the tools of Gentiles they despised to do their dirty work?

Jesus is Questioned by Pilate the First Time
John 18:33-38 [WEB]

33 Pilate therefore entered again into the Praetorium, called Jesus, and said to him, "Are you the King of the Jews?"

34 Jesus answered him, "Do you say this by yourself, or did others tell you about me?"

35 Pilate answered, "I'm not a Jew, am I? Your own nation and the chief priests delivered you to me. What have you done?"

36 Jesus answered, "My Kingdom is not of this world. If my Kingdom were of this world, then my servants would fight, that I wouldn't be delivered to the Jews. But now my Kingdom is not from here."

37 Pilate therefore said to him, "Are you a king then?"

Jesus answered, "You say that I am a king. For this reason I have been born, and for this reason I have come into the world, that I should testify to the truth. Everyone who is of the truth listens to my voice."

38 Pilate said to him, "What is truth?"

When he had said this, he went out again to the Jews, and said to them, "I find no basis for a charge against him.

Notes

1. Pilate knows that there is a distinction between political betrayal and theological betrayal or blasphemy.
2. **Pilate's question does not follow from ignorance of the meaning of truth. If Jesus is the King of Truth, he wants to know about this dominion.**

Questions for Reflection, Prayer, and Discussion

1. Why do you think Pilate takes this approach with his questioning?

2. Do you see Jesus' holiness having an effect upon Pilate in this passage?

Jesus Substitutes for Barabbas
John 18:39-40 [WEB]

39 But you have a custom that I should release someone to you at the Passover. Therefore, do you want me to release to you the King of the Jews?"
40 Then they all shouted again, saying, "Not this man, but Barabbas!" Now Barabbas was a robber.

Note

Pilate knows that Jesus is not guilty of a capital crime and declares it.

Questions for Reflection, Prayer, and Discussion

1. Of the sins of blasphemy and stealing, why do they seem to be treated differently?

2. Why do you think traditions, supposedly based upon Jewish law, seem so important to them?

Chapter Nineteen
Holiness Never Fails

Pilate Shows Possible Mercy
John 19:1-3 [WEB]

So Pilate then took Jesus and flogged him. 2 The soldiers twisted thorns into a crown and put it on his head, and dressed him in a purple garment. 3 They kept saying, "Hail, King of the Jews!" and they kept slapping him.

Notes

1. Though Jesus is innocent of political insurrection, Pilate had Jesus scourged, perhaps as an act of mercy to put the body of Christ in shock. In shock, Jesus might experience less pain, at least in Pilate's estimation. Although medical science was primitive during this period, the phenomenon was well known.
2. The addition of the crown of thorns is possibly an attempt to appease the crowd that wants Jesus to be crucified.

Questions for Reflection, Prayer, and Discussion

1. Is ordering the crucifixion the only way to avoid a riot at this point? Does Pilate have a realistic alternative?

2. What might be some symbolism in the crown of thorns?

Presentation to the Mob
John 19:4-7 [WEB]

4 Then Pilate went out again, and said to them, "Behold, I bring him out to you, that you may know that I find no basis for a charge against him."

5 Jesus therefore came out, wearing the crown of thorns and the purple garment. Pilate said to them, "Behold, the man!"

6 When therefore the chief priests and the officers saw him, they shouted, saying, "Crucify! Crucify!"

Pilate said to them, "Take him yourselves and crucify him, for I find no basis for a charge against him."

7 The Jews answered him, "We have a law, and by our law he ought to die, because he made himself the Son of God."

Notes
1. By inciting the riot, the leaders of the Temple probably anticipated Pilate's answer to the first accusation of political insurrection.
2. Pilate, like most Roman rulers, was highly superstitious and a skillful politician.

Questions for Reflection, Prayer, and Discussion
1. Was Pilate sending mixed signals with the crown of thorns, purple robe, and the denial of any capital offense on Jesus' part?

2. How was Jesus committing blasphemy by claiming to be The Son of God, according to the law?

READ Another Interrogation
John 19:8-11 [WEB]

8 When therefore Pilate heard this saying, he was more afraid. 9 He entered into the Praetorium again, and said to Jesus, "Where are you from?" But Jesus gave him no answer. 10 Pilate therefore said to him, "Aren't you speaking to me? Don't you know that I have power to release you and have power to crucify you?"

11 Jesus answered, "You would have no power at all against me, unless it were given to you from above. Therefore he who delivered me to you has greater sin."

Questions for Reflection, Prayer, and Discussion
1. What significance might this conversation have for John, that he includes it for his audience?

2. Do you think the High Priest accepted responsibility for Jesus' death? Why?

Priorities Question
John 19:12-16a [WEB]

12 At this, Pilate was seeking to release him, but the Jews cried out, saying, "If you release this man, you aren't Caesar's friend! Everyone who makes himself a king speaks against Caesar!"

13 When Pilate therefore heard these words, he brought Jesus out and sat down on the judgment seat at a place called "The Pavement", but in Hebrew, "Gabbatha." 14 Now it was the Preparation Day of the Passover, at about the sixth hour. He said to the Jews, "Behold, your King!"

15 They cried out, "Away with him! Away with him! Crucify him!"

Pilate said to them, "Shall I crucify your King?"

The chief priests answered, "We have no king but Caesar!"

16a So then he delivered him to them to be crucified.

Questions for Reflection, Prayer, and Discussion

1. What is Pilate's main priority in his political role?

2. What is the main priority of the temple leaders?

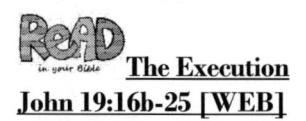

The Execution
John 19:16b-25 [WEB]

16b So they took Jesus and led him away. 17 He went out, bearing his cross, to the place called "The Place of a Skull", which is called in Hebrew, "Golgotha", 18 where they crucified him, and with him two others, on either side one, and Jesus in the middle. 19 Pilate wrote a title also, and put it on the cross. There was written, "JESUS OF NAZARETH, THE KING OF THE JEWS." 20 Therefore many of the Jews read this title, for the place where Jesus was crucified was near the city; and it was written in Hebrew, in Latin, and in Greek. 21 The chief priests of the Jews therefore said to Pilate, "Don't write, 'The King of the Jews,' but, 'he said, "I am King of the Jews." ' "

22 Pilate answered, "What I have written, I have written."

23 Then the soldiers, when they had crucified Jesus, took his garments and made four parts, to every soldier a part; and also the tunic. Now the tunic was without seam, woven from the top throughout. 24 Then they said to one another, "Let's not tear it, but cast lots for it to decide whose it will be," that the Scripture might be fulfilled, which says, "They parted my garments among them. They cast lots for my clothing." Therefore the soldiers did these things.

25 But standing by Jesus' cross were his mother, his mother's sister, Mary the wife of Clopas, and Mary Magdalene.

Notes

1. The execution site, Golgotha, is a cliff just outside the city wall that has a profile that resembles a skull.
2. Pilate's contemptuous attitude toward the Jewish leadership [14] is reflected in the inscription. [19]

Questions for Reflection, Prayer, and Discussion

1. What aspects of this account of the execution reflect John's unique point of view, compared to the other three gospels?

2. When you read this account, what does John mention that is the most important thing to your experience of faith?

ReAD Bequests
John 19:26-27 [WEB]

26 Therefore when Jesus saw his mother, and the disciple whom he loved standing there, he said to his mother, "Woman, behold, your son!" 27 Then he said to the disciple, "Behold, your mother!" From that hour, the disciple took her to his own home.

Questions for Reflection, Prayer, and Discussion

1. Does this passage give us insight as to the identity of the author of the gospel? Is it important?

2. Do you experience a kinship with Jesus' humanity here?

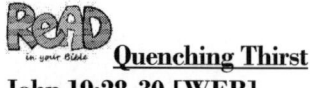

Quenching Thirst
John 19:28-30 [WEB]

28 After this, Jesus, seeing that all things were now finished, that the Scripture might be fulfilled, said, "I am thirsty!" 29 Now a vessel full of vinegar was set there; so they put a sponge full of the vinegar on hyssop, and held it at his mouth. 30 When Jesus therefore had received the vinegar, he said, "It is finished!" Then he bowed his head and gave up his spirit.

Notes
1. The cry of thirst and its response fulfills Psalm 69:21.
2. At last, Jesus was finished with all that God had sent him to do. He was in control and surrendered His life for all humankind.

A Question for Reflection and Discussion
When witnessing to his readers, why do you suppose John does not supply the anecdotes concerning Jesus' death as found in the other gospels?

The Body Is Pierced
John 19:31-37 [WEB]

31 Therefore the Jews, because it was the Preparation Day, so that the bodies wouldn't remain on the cross on the Sabbath (for that Sabbath was a special one), asked of Pilate that their legs might be broken and that they might be taken away. 32 Therefore the soldiers came and broke the legs of the first and of the other who was crucified with him; 33 but when they came to Jesus and saw that he was already dead,

they didn't break his legs. 34 However, one of the soldiers pierced his side with a spear, and immediately blood and water came out. 35 He who has seen has testified, and his testimony is true. He knows that he tells the truth, that you may believe. 36 For these things happened that the Scripture might be fulfilled, "A bone of him will not be broken." 37 Again another Scripture says, "They will look on him whom they pierced."

Notes

1. Breaking the legs of these crucified was an act of mercy as the resulting shock to the system would hasten death. Jesus had already been in shock over the flogging and had already died.
2. The mention of blood and water by John may be a confirmation of the humanity of Jesus, but it may also indicate references to baptism and the Lord's Supper.

Questions for Reflection, Prayer, and Discussion

1. As John witnesses to you, how does this passage affect your images of Jesus both as a man and as Messiah?

2. How could Christians and non-Christians be impressed in the same ways or different ways by this passage?

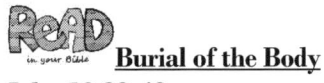

ReAD Burial of the Body
John 19:38-42

38 After these things, Joseph of Arimathaea, being a disciple of Jesus, but secretly for fear of the Jews, asked of Pilate that he might take away Jesus' body. Pilate gave him permission. He came therefore and took away his body. 39 Nicodemus, who at first came to Jesus by night, also came bringing a mixture of myrrh and aloes, about a hundred Roman pounds. 40 So they took Jesus' body, and bound it in linen cloths with the spices, as the custom of the Jews is to bury. 41 Now in the place where he was crucified there was a garden. In the garden was a new tomb in which no man had ever yet been laid. 42 Then, because of the Jews' Preparation Day (for the tomb was near at hand), they laid Jesus there.

Notes

1. Whoever touched the body was ritually impure and therefore unable to take part in the celebration of the Passover.
2. Myrrh, in combination with crushed aloe, was often used for embalming.
3. In weight, one hundred Roman pounds would be about 75 pounds avoirdupois today.

Questions for Reflection, Prayer, and Discussion

1. What kinds of risks were involved in their actions at this time?

2. Considering the timing of the Passover pressure, what do you think of these people's resourcefulness?

3. Since no one was considering resurrection at this time, what do you think might be going through their minds?

Chapter Twenty
Holiness Can Astonish

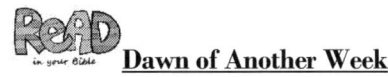

READ: Dawn of Another Week
John 20:1 [WEB]

Now on the first day of the week, Mary Magdalene went early, while it was still dark, to the tomb, and saw that the stone had been taken away from the tomb.

Note

John does not deal with the details of the number of days which have passed since the death of Jesus, but merely indicates that it is Sunday that the tomb is discovered empty.

READ: Peter & John Get the News
John 20:2 [WEB]

2 Therefore she ran and came to Simon Peter and to the other disciple whom Jesus loved, and said to them, "They have taken away the Lord out of the tomb, and we don't know where they have laid him!"

Note

The empty tomb emphasizes the resurrection rather than simple immortality.

READ: Peter & John Investigate
John 20:3-10 [WEB]

3 Therefore Peter and the other disciple went out, and they went toward the tomb. 4 They both ran together. The other disciple outran Peter and came to the tomb first. 5 Stooping and looking in, he saw the linen cloths lying there; yet he didn't enter in. 6 Then Simon Peter came, following him, and entered into the tomb. He saw the linen cloths lying, 7 and the cloth that had been on his head, not lying with the linen cloths, but rolled up in a place by itself. 8 So then the other disciple who came first to the tomb also entered in, and he saw and believed. 9 For as yet they didn't know the Scripture, that he must rise from the dead. 10 So the disciples went away again to their own homes.

A Question for Reflection, Prayer, and Discussion

Of the women, Peter, and John, how do their faith actions impress you differently?

Mary Encounters the Risen Christ
John 20:11-17 [WEB]

11 But Mary was standing outside at the tomb weeping. So as she wept, she stooped and looked into the tomb, 12 and she saw two angels in white sitting, one at the head and one at the feet, where the body of Jesus had lain. 13 They asked her, "Woman, why are you weeping?"

She said to them, "Because they have taken away my Lord, and I don't know where they have laid him." 14 When she had said this, she turned around and saw Jesus standing, and didn't know that it was Jesus.

15 Jesus said to her, "Woman, why are you weeping? Who are you looking for?"

She, supposing him to be the gardener, said to him, "Sir, if you have carried him away, tell me where you have laid him, and I will take him away."

16 Jesus said to her, "Mary."

She turned and said to him, "Rabboni!" which is to say, "Teacher!"

17 Jesus said to her, "Don't hold me, for I haven't yet ascended to my Father; but go to my brothers and tell them, 'I am ascending to my Father and your Father, to my God and your God.' "

Notes
1. In her grief, she does not at first even look at the face of the man who speaks to her, for it does not occur to her that it could be Jesus.
2. In her tears, Mary does not seem to wonder at the presence of the angels.

Questions for Reflection, Prayer, and Discussion
1. What are some reasons for this story being so important for John in the encouragement of Christians in their walk with the Christ of faith?

2. Do you think Mary's encounter with Jesus helped her grow towards His holiness? Why?

Read in your Bible — Mary Witnesses
John 20:18 [WEB]

18 Mary Magdalene came and told the disciples that she had seen the Lord, and that he had said these things to her.

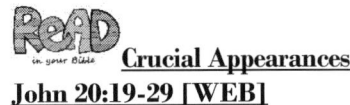

Read in your Bible — Crucial Appearances
John 20:19-29 [WEB]

19 When therefore it was evening on that day, the first day of the week, and when the doors were locked where the disciples were assembled, for fear of the Jews, Jesus came and stood in the middle and said to them, "Peace be to you."

20 When he had said this, he showed them his hands and his side. The disciples therefore were glad when they saw the Lord. 21 Jesus therefore said to them again, "Peace be to you. As the Father has sent me, even so I send you." 22 When he had said this, he breathed on them, and said to them, "Receive the Holy Spirit! 23 If you forgive anyone's sins, they have been forgiven them. If you retain anyone's sins, they have been retained."

24 But Thomas, one of the twelve, called Didymus, wasn't with them when Jesus came. 25 The other disciples therefore said to him, "We have seen the Lord!"

But he said to them, "Unless I see in his hands the print of the nails, put my finger into the print of the nails, and put my hand into his side, I will not believe."

26 After eight days, again his disciples were inside and Thomas was with them. Jesus came, the doors being locked, and stood in the middle, and said, "Peace be to you." 27 Then he said to Thomas, "Reach here your finger, and see my hands. Reach here your hand, and put it into my side. Don't be unbelieving, but believing."

28 Thomas answered him, "My Lord and my God!"

29 Jesus said to him, "Because you have seen me, you have believed. Blessed are those who have not seen and have believed."

Notes

1. John uses both appearances to underline Jesus' bodily resurrection. An apostasy at the time the gospel was written was that only Jesus' spirit was resurrected, and the controversy continues today among some theologians.
2. For John, this is where Jesus bestows the Holy Spirit.

Questions for Reflection, Prayer, and Discussion

1. Why was Jesus' giving of the Holy Spirit important to them?

2. Considering the story of Thomas, do you understand the doubts of today's followers of Jesus who doubt the bodily resurrection of Jesus?

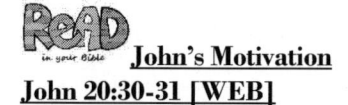

READ: John's Motivation
John 20:30-31 [WEB]

30 Therefore Jesus did many other signs in the presence of his disciples, which are not written in this book; 31 but these are written that you may believe that Jesus is the Christ, the Son of God, and that believing you may have life in his name.

Notes

1. The Gospel of John is the only one of the four which gives internal evidence of the author of the testimony.
2. John's gospel is also the only one that has a stated purpose, although the writer of Luke alludes to a purpose in his introductions to his gospel account and to Acts.

Chapter Twenty-one

READ **Disciples Go Fishing**

John 21:1-3 [WEB]

1 After these things, Jesus revealed himself again to the disciples at the sea of Tiberias. He revealed himself this way. 2 Simon Peter, Thomas called Didymus, Nathanael of Cana in Galilee, and the sons of Zebedee, and two others of his disciples were together. 3 Simon Peter said to them, "I'm going fishing."

Note

Evidently, the expectation of the anointing of the Holy Spirit possibly caused the disciples to become restless.

READ **Jesus Acts as Spotter for a Final Encounter**

John 21:4-8 [WEB]

4 But when day had already come, Jesus stood on the beach; yet the disciples didn't know that it was Jesus. 5 Jesus therefore said to them, "Children, have you anything to eat?"

They answered him, "No."

6 He said to them, "Cast the net on the right side of the boat, and you will find some."

They cast it therefore, and now they weren't able to draw it in for the multitude of fish. 7 That disciple therefore whom Jesus loved said to Peter, "It's the Lord!"

So when Simon Peter heard that it was the Lord, he wrapped his coat around himself (for he was naked), and threw himself into the sea. 8 But the other disciples came in the little boat (for they were not far from the land, but about two hundred cubits away), dragging the net full of fish.

Notes

1. Jesus' use of the Greek term translated children may be likened to the term "boys" or "friends."
2. Early in the morning, fishers sometimes had observers on the shore who had a better view of the fish.
3. John is the first to recognize Jesus in the early light, and he tells Peter and the others.

Questions for Reflection, Prayer, and Discussion

1. If you saw a dark figure in the first light, offering you help, what would you think?

2. Once you saw it was the Lord, would you swim ashore as Peter did or help the others row the boat?

Read: Eating Is a Reminder of Jesus' Full Humanity
John 21:9-14 [WEB]

9 So when they got out on the land, they saw a fire of coals there, with fish and bread laid on it. 10 Jesus said to them, "Bring some of the fish which you have just caught."

11 Simon Peter went up, and drew the net to land, full of one hundred fifty-three great fish. Even though there were so many, the net wasn't torn.

12 Jesus said to them, "Come and eat breakfast!"

None of the disciples dared inquire of him, "Who are you?" knowing that it was the Lord.

13 Then Jesus came and took the bread, gave it to them, and the fish likewise.
14 This is now the third time that Jesus was revealed to his disciples after he had risen from the dead.

Note
Note that the charcoal fire is already there with the fish already cooking, with the bread being preheated.

A Question for Reflection, Prayer, and Discussion
What are some possible implications in His already having fish on a fire when they come ashore?

Read: Feeding as Example
John 21:15-19 [WEB]

15 So when they had eaten their breakfast, Jesus said to Simon Peter, "Simon, son of Jonah, do you love me more than these?"

He said to him, "Yes, Lord; you know that I have affection for you."

He said to him, "Feed my lambs." 16 He said to him again a second time, "Simon, son of Jonah, do you love me?"

He said to him, "Yes, Lord; you know that I have affection for you."

He said to him, "Tend my sheep." 17 He said to him the third time, "Simon, son of Jonah, do you have affection for me?"

Peter was grieved because he asked him the third time, "Do you have affection for me?" He said to him, "Lord, you know everything. You know that I have affection for you."

Jesus said to him, "Feed my sheep. 18 Most certainly I tell you, when you were young, you dressed yourself and walked where you wanted to. But when you are old, you will stretch out your hands, and another will dress you and carry you where you don't want to go."

19 Now he said this, signifying by what kind of death he would glorify God. When he had said this, he said to him, "Follow me."

Notes
1. The three questions are in line with Peter's three denials.
2. Tradition says that Nero in the late 60s CE martyred Peter in Rome.

Questions for Reflection, Prayer, and Discussion
1. If you were in Peter's shoes, would you be grieved by the time of the third question?

2. Why do you suppose John includes this conversation in his witness to the Christian community?

About the Author: John 21:20-23 [WEB]

20 Then Peter, turning around, saw a disciple following. This was the disciple whom Jesus loved, the one who had also leaned on Jesus' breast at the supper and asked, "Lord, who is going to betray you?" 21 Peter, seeing him, said to Jesus, "Lord, what about this man?"

22 Jesus said to him, "If I desire that he stay until I come, what is that to you? You follow me." 23 This saying therefore went out among the brothers that this disciple wouldn't die. Yet Jesus didn't say to him that he wouldn't die, but, "If I desire that he stay until I come, what is that to you?"

A Question for Reflection, Prayer, and Discussion

What rumors might John be dealing with here?

ReAD — A Final Note
John 21:24-25 [WEB]

24 This is the disciple who testifies about these things, and wrote these things. We know that his witness is true. 25 There are also many other things which Jesus did, which if they would all be written, I suppose that even the world itself wouldn't have room for the books that would be written.

A Question for Reflection, Prayer, and Discussion

Considering these two verses, along with John 20:30-31, what impressions do you have of the author of this gospel?

Questions for Further Reflection and Discussion

1. In the final scene of John's gospel, Jesus has not yet ascended into heaven. The Holy Spirit, the promised *advocate*, has not been given with power at Pentecost. List some of the ways that the remaining eleven are ready to proceed with their mission and live lives of holiness.

2. As you faithfully follow Jesus, try to be like Him, and grow towards His holiness, what aspects of Jesus' life and character do you hope will be (or already are) within yourself?

Available at Amazon

Other Books by James J. Stewart

Christian Inspiration, Bible Study, and Poetry

366 Brief Prayers for Your Church Community
[Daily prayers]

*Faith and Yosemite:
Fourth Edition*
[Christian poetry with pictures of Yosemite]

Faith Fuel
[Meditations on the Christian faith and life]

Lasting Love
[Short Biographical Sketches]

Living for Jesus
[A Gospels Study Guide for Couples and Small Groups]

*Deliberately
Growing Spiritually*
[A five-year Bible reading program.]

Seed Thoughts for Christian Prayer and Meditation
[Workbook]

Single Sentence Sermons
[Workbook for growing faith]

Walking in Faith
[Much of the same poetry as Faith and Yosemite but without pictures]

Spiritually Growing Through Prayer
[Personal piety and spiritual growth through prayer]

In Jesus' Name
[Praying Effectively]

Christian Fiction

A Man, A Woman, and a Cat
[A cheetah/Puma crossbreed brings together an architect and a famous actress.]

A Marriage of Miracles
[God sets up a whirlwind romance & fills two people's lives with miracles]

The Camera Doctors
[Two people meet on top a famous mountain, and romance ensues.]

Casting Lots
[Christian romance and adventure set in the near future]

*Christian Romances
in the Foothills*
An anthology of Tom's Town, Soul Mates, & The Camera Doctors

Deborah
[Similar to the Bible's Deborah, she is a prophet. God tells her to use a hacker to bring down political corruption]

Elijah
[God uses a retired pastor to prophesy with national and worldwide repercussions.]

Empty Tomb, Full Hearts
[A Selection of Testimonies Among Those Who Saw the Risen Christ]

An Extensive Life
[The life story of a man who lived more than four hundred years.]

The First Lady
[A brilliant musician and a brilliant astrophysicist stumble into politics, and they write new chapters of history.

The Gaardian Saga
[Christian science fiction fantasy involving God in a major role.]

God, Love, and Stargazing
God prepares two people for both romance and divine service.

A Nation Transformed
[A future tale of God intervening in the USA with miracles.

A Second Call to Serve
[A tenth-generation pastor and his second wife accept a call to build a church from scratch.]

Prayer Warriors
[Urban adventures in a near-future continuation of Casting Lots]
Soul Mates
[Romance, the same setting as Tom's Town]

This World Is Not My Home
[Together since high school, they separate to find love with others.]
Tom's Town
[Small town life and Christian romance]
<u>The Warrior and the Prophet</u>
<u>*[God has surprises and blessings for newlyweds]*</u>

<u>Yosemite Picture Books</u>

Ever-Changing Yosemite Valley
[Yosemite Valley is a glacially carved valley. Moment by moment, scenes change.]

Faith and Yosemite Fourth Edition
[Pictures of Yosemite National Park, with poetry about the Christian faith]

Portraits of El Capitan
[El Capitan rises 3000 feet above the floor of Yosemite Valley at the west end]

Portraits of Half Dome
[Half Dome marks the east end of Yosemite Valley]

A Sense of Wonder: Yosemite
[A Christian poem about Yosemite, illustrated with pictures]

Starlight Over Yosemite
[Large pictures of Yosemite taken at night]

Yosemite Textures and Shadows
[High-definition photographs of Yosemite Valley, depicting all seasons, both day and night.]

Made in the USA
Columbia, SC
31 October 2021